MONEY SKILLS FOR TEENS
AND
FINANCIAL LITERACY FOR YOUNG ADULTS

2 Books in 1

Learn Successful Money Management and Personal Finance Skills to Go From Zero to Financial Security Already in Your 20s

EMILY CARTER

TABLE OF CONTENTS

FINANCIAL LITERACY FOR YOUNG ADULTS

YOUR FREE GIFT

To really make the most out of your life, and to succeed in it, it's crucial to never stop learning. To further develop your knowledge of important life skills, I've got something for you... something you can really be excited about!

As a way of saying thank you for your purchase, I want to offer you some BONUSES completely FREE of charge:

To get instant access, just go to:

https://lifeskillbooks.com

Here's just a glimpse of what is included:

BONUS 1

91 Easy Ways to Save Money This Year: Practical Steps for Smarter Spending

Inside this checklist, you will discover...

- Surprisingly simple ways to start saving money already today!
- The Clever Money-Saving Techniques for shopping that you most likely have not discovered yet.
- And much more! 91 tips in total. That's a lot.

BONUS 2

101 Fast Fixes to Boost Your Credit Score:
Your 101-Step Roadmap to Credit Success

Inside this 71-page!! ebook, you will discover...

- Gain a solid understanding of the fundamentals of credit scores and how they impact your financial health, setting the stage for informed decision-making.

- Identify common mistakes that can negatively impact your credit score, some of which you are most likely doing yourself!

- And finally... learn to build a perfect credit score for yourself, even if you're starting from the bottom.

BONUS 3

Automated Money Management Playbook: Simplified Guide to Hands-Off Financial Management

Inside this useful playbook, you will discover...

- The benefits of automated finances and why you should start automating your finances already today.
- The 7 Must-have tools for seamless automation.
- Invaluable tips and tricks for automating all your transactions from paying bills to retirement investing and everything in between.

Now, go visit the website below for instant access to these three and several other amazing bonuses. Completely free of charge.

https://lifeskillbooks.com

MONEY SKILLS
FOR TEENS

*These Are The Things
About Money Management
and Personal Finance
You Must Know But They
Didn't Teach You in School*

EMILY CARTER

INTRODUCTION

You are at a stage in your life where you need to learn as much as you can and prepare yourself for what is coming. Finances and financial literacy, in general, are very important parts of being an adult, and making the right financial decisions can set you up for a great life. Being financially literate will teach you important lessons that many adults only learn later in life after they've already made a few mistakes. This is not to say that these mistakes cannot be reversed, but they take time and effort, and you certainly want your adult life to go as smoothly as you possibly can. While there are many different aspects of life that we can't control, finances aren't one of them. We can act on them and turn things around.

By understanding finances, you can learn the differences between your needs and your wants, the real value of money, how money can work in your favor, and how you can avoid crippling debt. Your future and your financial independence are coming, and it's always best to be prepared for them.

The main goal of this book is to encourage you to take control of your finances from the very start so you can build enough wealth to live a peaceful life (at least when it comes to your finances) and to prepare you for what's coming. This book is structured in a way to make you understand the very basics first, such as what money is or how to make money as a teenager. Then, once you know the basics, I'll move on to more complex subjects such as banking and financial services; what is budgeting and how can it help; what is credit or debt management; the intricacies of insurance and how it can provide security for you, and your loved ones; and how caring about retirement now can help you later in life.

This is the beginning of your journey, but if you make good decisions now, you will have a much easier life in the future.

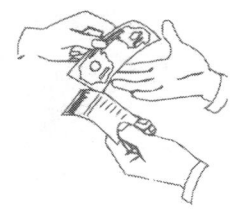

CHAPTER 1

UNDERSTANDING MONEY

> *A wise person should have money in their head, but not in their heart.*
>
> — *Jonathan Swift*

When we think about money, we think about notes and coins and, more recently, numbers in our banking apps that allow us to pay for products or services that we want or need. But in a sober way, money is a system of exchange that allows us to get services or goods for a certain value in money. The monetary system was created to replace another, older system that you might have heard about called barter trading, which was used thousands of years ago. In this system, money wasn't involved, so if you wanted a service or good, you'd have to exchange it for another service or good. Let's say you lived during those times and you wanted someone to come fix your fence; in return, you'd give him goods, which at the time could be eggs, a cow, or milk. Or, if you could perform a service such as shoemaking, maybe you'd fix or even make new shoes for the person fixing your fence.

So, in other words, money is an asset, in this case, a liquid asset (because it can easily be transformed into cash; for instance, if you withdraw $10 from an ATM, you're turning money into cash), that allows us to make transfers of value in an easy way between two people or organizations.

In this chapter, we are going to understand the role of money in our lives, what exactly the value of money is and its impact on our personal finance decisions, and how we can develop a healthy money mindset and set attainable financial goals.

The Role of Money in Our Lives

In our lives, money is important because it allows us to have a better quality of life by enabling us to have options in the things we do in our day-to-day activities, both short- and long-term. Having enough money allows us to have more security and freedom. It's safe to say that the amount of money we have can dictate our lifestyle.

It's also true that money, at times, can have negative effects on people, but it largely depends on their actions. In fact, our actions regarding the money we collect are crucial; whether it is how we spend it, save it, or invest it, these actions have an impact on our lives. The store value of money is crucial, allowing us to keep it and use it later on. This ability allows people and businesses to plan for the future, such as retirement, purchasing a property, or buying a car. Money can also be used as a medium to account for and give value to services and goods. If a pair of shoes costs $100, this is money being used as a unit of account to allow us to understand the value of the pair of shoes compared to other things. It's extremely easy for us to compare different items and services and make financial decisions.

Besides that, money can also be used in more complex contexts, such as a vital part of financial markets or financial institutions such as banks. In the case of banks, their business is solely based on money, especially the loan and the store of money, while investors use the money to purchase financial instruments such as bonds or stocks.

Money allows us to pay for the most basic things, such as healthcare, food, and housing. But it can also be a source of stress, happiness, status, or power. Whether we like it or not, even though we often hear that money is not everything (and it certainly isn't), it's a crucial part of our lives and our society, and without it, the world would be a completely different place.

Moreover, money can also have an impact on emotional, mental, and even physical well-being. This often stems from a lack of it rather than an abundance. Stress-related money issues can come from difficulties in paying bills or providing basic needs to us or our families, which can lead to anxiety, stress, and even depression. The constant pursuit of money can have an effect on our happiness, even if we have enough of it. It comes down to a never-ending cycle of permanent desire and chasing material things. And so having a good balance between what we want and what we have is essential for our own health. At the end of the day, money is simply a tool; it can't buy happiness or fulfillment, and it can only fulfill these momentarily. While the scope of this book is about money and all the things we can accomplish with it, it's important to understand that there's more to life.

How to Develop a Healthy Money Mindset and Set Up Your Financial Goals

Now that this is out of the way let's get down to what this book is about. Developing a healthy money mindset and setting financial goals is the first step to understanding money and being able to manage it.

Did you know that one in five people says they are overwhelmed by debt? This is according to a survey done by the Money Advice Service, which can have a negative impact on people's health. This comes from the constant worry that occupies our minds, which in turn can inflate the issue, making it look like it's impossible to resolve (FarmWell, n.d.). Ignoring the problem is probably our first reaction. I know it was mine before I learned the hard way that we shouldn't simply ignore these issues, as oftentimes, they simply don't go away and come back way worse than before. As hard as it might seem, we need to look the problem in the eye and try to understand what we can do to overcome it. What are the steps that you need to take to make this problem go away? Everybody's different, and so we have different issues, but by developing a healthy money mindset, you become a lot less scared of these problems, and you will have a clear head on what you need to do next.

Some of the most common barriers when it comes to developing this mindset are how to properly manage money. This can stem from a lack of knowledge, a lack of confidence, or even debt. Although all of these can be worked out. One other problem when establishing a healthy money mindset is the too-often limiting thought about money and finance in general. The problem here is that these thoughts often limit the things we can do. You might not even realize it, but things such as "I don't make enough money to be able to save" or "I will never be able to get out of debt." Even if you don't actively think about them, they live in your subconscious. You need to get rid of these limitations, or you will never be able to develop a healthy money mindset. The first thing you have to do is identify when these thoughts come and push them back. This might take a little getting used to because we've been living with these thoughts for a while, and it's hard to break the habit, but when you feel them coming, try to hold them by looking at the evidence. For instance, how is it even possible that you will never be out of debt? It doesn't make sense, especially if you have a plan to pay off that debt. Looking at the real evidence in these cases, you'll find that many limitations are quite absurd. The most important aspect of developing a healthy money mindset is to have control. If you feel overwhelmed or out of control, then you feel more stressed.

In the following section, I will talk about many different techniques, such as setting financial goals and others that will make you more open to the development of your healthy mindset. One that I tend to recommend is to make a plan and create a budget. There are many different tools that can help you do that, and you can even find free templates online. But tools like apps will do most of the work for you and help you take control of your finances. Sometimes simply talking to someone can help you manage your financial stress too. Most of us try to keep everything for ourselves, which is often not a great solution. Communicating with someone that you trust can have a calming effect on you and put things into better perspective. Taking inventory of your finances might be a boring job to do, but it can really help you understand where your money is going and get control over your finances. Again, there are many different tools and apps that can help you track your expenses automatically, such as Mint, Personal Capital, or PocketGuard.

Steps to Develop a Healthy Money Mindset

One of the hardest things someone has to overcome when developing a healthy mindset is forgiving their past financial mistakes. It's way too easy to get hung up on the mistakes we've made and constantly think about what we should have done instead. But the past is the past, and there's nothing we can do to change it. We need to stop wasting our mental focus on things that we can no longer control and focus on the things we can, such as future financial decisions. Focus your money decisions on things that you can control and not on things of the past. Your success is ahead of you.

It's also important to be able to identify the emotions you usually have when it comes to money. This way, you can try to change that emotional state as well as the thoughts that might trigger those negative emotions. A good exercise to identify these thoughts and emotions is to write down what you're feeling after each transaction for a week. At the end of the week, take a look over, and you'll find the necessary purchases and those that aren't. For instance, if you buy a pair of shoes and at the moment of purchase you believe this will bring you joy, at the end of the week, you might feel differently and know that the purchase might have been an impulse purchase. This is also a great way to understand your spending habits and how emotionally connected you are to your purchases. Don't let your purchases be guided by your emotions; think rationally when it comes to financial decisions.

We often compare ourselves to others, and it's not only in financial terms. Either way is a losing game, and it's something that we should try to steer away from. These types of comparisons are never accurate, especially because we often compare ourselves with someone who is apparently much better off than we are and that we know nothing about. This is even more abundant in our social media-filled lives, where often people just post their highlights or only the things they want you to see. Looking at social media posts, for instance, you might see someone enjoying a beach day in the Caribbean, but you don't know how much debt they might have incurred to be there or if they owe money to family or friends. Chances are you will never find out the truth because they won't post it on their social media. Now, when you do these comparisons, you know everything about you, the good and the bad, and that makes it an unfair comparison to make. Even when you compare yourself with people that you know, it's still an unfair comparison because the circumstances aren't similar, even though you might know them a little. After all, even if you realize that they are better off than you are, what do you have to gain from that? You will likely become quite discouraged with yourself, which doesn't help anyone. You should be developing a healthy mindset, which you can't do if you focus on all the negative sides of it. In order to build a healthy money mindset, you have to solely focus on yourself and on achieving your goals. What others do or don't shouldn't be on your mind.

Forming good habits, in general, is not something that will happen overnight, so you have to work on them continuously. This is exactly the same when trying to form good financial habits. You should take some time to do your budget every week, or at least every month, and go over the bills and your spending habits too. This is the only way you will be able to find out what can be improved. Avoiding doing this is probably the worst thing you can do because if there are any problems, they won't go away anyway. Make sure you create good financial habits and work on them, such as making a budget. These habits are the foundation of your personal finances today and in the future.

However, when creating a budget, don't restrain yourself too much, at least not at the beginning. You have to create one that brings you happiness and that you're comfortable with. This often means not restricting yourself from enjoying life. Although you might have to limit this. For instance, instead of dining out every day, you might have to cut it back to twice a week. However, all budgets are different, and we are going through the different budget strategies in the chapter dedicated to budgeting later in the book.

Setting Financial Goals

While the way you set financial goals will differ as you grow, there's always a structure that you might want to follow. For instance, if you're just starting out, your main concern should be focusing on quick wins so you get the feel for it and understand that financial goals are indeed attainable. Starting slowly is important to keep your motivation levels high and pursue other, more ambitious goals. When starting anything, sometimes we have the fear of failing, which often prevents us from reaching certain goals. However, if you're not going to try, you will certainly not accomplish anything at all. For instance, while saving $1000 might seem like a daunting goal, it's much easier to save $200 or $300, and this is where you should start. This will also help you steer away from procrastination and continue to set more goals as the current ones get accomplished.

Having the freedom to set your own goals is great, but you also need to understand the costs and benefits of the goals you want to set. For instance, if you want to take a summer course that will cost you money, how will taking that course benefit you in the long run? Are you going to be able to improve your financial situation because of that course? If so, it's certainly a good investment. Also, it's important to remember that not all costs are monetary; some of them take up some of your time. You have to consider all of the pros and cons associated with those.

Financial goals come in three distinct lengths: short, medium, and long. To determine the length of your goals, you have to look at the cost of the goal, or how much you will have to save, the resources you have to use, and your motivations, since the higher the motivation, the more likely you are to accomplish your goals. But, as a rule of thumb, a short-term financial goal is anything that takes a maximum of a month to accomplish, a medium-term goal is anything between one and three months, and a long-term goal is anything over three months. When setting your goals, it's important that you have a mix of these three so you always have something to look forward to and keep you motivated, but I will develop this in the chapter about budgeting.

Understanding money is the first step to acquiring the necessary skills that will help you as you go from your teenage years into your young adult years, and you will have to rely more on how you manage your money. As we've seen, money is an integral part of everybody's lives, and so making the right decisions is absolutely essential for you to continue to prosper financially. For that, starting with developing a healthy money mindset and understanding how to set attainable financial goals is essential.

In the following chapter, I'll go through the different ways you can start making money and how you can develop skills that will be useful to you later on in your career.

CHAPTER 2

MAKING MONEY

> Opportunity is missed by most people because it is dressed in overalls and looks like work.
>
> — *Thomas Edison*

N ow we get to the good part: how can you make money as a teenager? Well, I can tell you right away that there are many different options you can take, and I'm certain you will find some that you will be happy with.

The Different Ways You Can Make Money

Usually, there are three types of work you can do to earn money as a teenager: part-time jobs, freelancing, or entrepreneurship. You might wonder what exactly the difference is between freelancing and entrepreneurship, and while there are definitely some similarities, there are some crucial differences. I believe the main difference between these two is that a freelancer is hired to work or do some tasks by other companies, while entrepreneurs create companies and manage them. While entrepreneurs come up with an idea and develop it into a business model, freelancers give more value to their skills and try to hone them as best they can.

While entrepreneurs can sell products and services behind a business to customers, freelancers sell their services and skills to other businesses. Let's delve into it a little more.

Part-Time Jobs

While you're under the age of 18, you can't apply for every single job, but there's quite a lot to choose from, especially if you're looking for a part-time job. Whether you want to work after school, during the weekends, or throughout the summer, I'm going to give you some of the most common part-time jobs you are allowed to do.

For example, babysitting is a very common job for teenagers. I understand it's not for everyone since you might not have the patience to take care of younger kids, but either way, this is a very well-paid job. I'm sure you're familiar with what the job requires you to do, such as looking after young children while their parents are away. To apply for these jobs, while it is not strictly necessary, I always recommend having first aid training because little accidents happen, especially with kids, and you want to make sure you have that covered. If you have a younger sibling, then I'm sure you have some experience taking care of kids; if not, you don't have any previous references to give. I suggest you go around the neighborhoods to find families that you know and talk to them to understand if they would be interested in getting a babysitter.

A sales assistant, sometimes called a sales associate or a shop assistant, is also a job that many teenagers can do, and the advantage of these types of jobs is that you can choose to work in many different industries. Maybe you're interested in fashion, and so working in a clothes shop might be an interesting experience for you, or maybe a video game shop or a pet shop. The options are many, and that's the beauty of being a shop assistant. There's usually some manual work alongside customer service, but it gives you a lot of great experience interacting with people, and it's usually a lot of fun. Many businesses in the retail industry staff teenagers, so you might also find interesting people your age. If you like to interact with customers, then becoming a shop assistant can be something that you will really enjoy.

Barista is another great first job if you want to earn some money. If you already know how to make any type of coffee, that's great, but in most coffee shops, that's not a requirement, and it's a skill you might be able to learn within a week or two. However, the most important skill to have as a barista is your customer service skills. If you are a natural at talking to people and are cheerful, you will love working as a barista. Most of those places also give you some training if you're not proficient at talking to people but want to learn how to interact and be skilled at customer service.

If you enjoy working outdoors, then perhaps you might want to find a part-time job as a gardener. Now, there are many different things to learn when you become a gardener, but as a teenager starting your first job, you won't need to know everything professional gardeners do, plus, you are likely to work with a more experienced gardener, so you can learn. There are also easy gardening jobs that you can do, such as trimming edges, mowing lawns, clipping bushes, watering, or planting. Again, perhaps the easiest way to start making money as a gardener is to go around your neighborhood and ask if they need a gardener for small jobs. While your parents might already have some of the most basic tools, as you progress and continue to do the job, you might want to add a few more tools or upgrade the ones you use to make your job easier.

Being a fast food worker is a very cliche job for a teenager, but it's an easy one to find, and you can make great money even working part-time. Now, most employees in these types of jobs have to be on their feet all day, and that's perhaps the hardest part of the job. But if you can do it, fast food restaurants tend to have very flexible hours that you can accommodate with the other things that you do throughout your day.

If you love animals, dog walking might be the right job for you. In fact, it may not even feel like a job at all. It's quite a popular job for teenagers who like the outdoors and feel confident around dogs. Many dog owners simply don't have the time to walk their pets, but they deeply care about them and have no problem spending money to give their furry friends the best treatment. For you, it all comes down to establishing some good clients, and you can even walk more than one dog, which will increase your income exponentially. This is also a job that is quite flexible, so you can manage your time better.

In recent years, the food delivery industry changed its way of delivering, which allowed teenagers who didn't yet have a full driver's license to do the job by riding bicycles or mopeds. This type of transportation is more evident in large cities with a lot of traffic, where bike couriers have become the norm. While earning money, you might also get a chance to exercise if you ride a bicycle. The amount of money you can make in these jobs is dependent on the number of hours, of course, but also on how efficient you are in quickly getting the food to the customers, where you are then rated. If you do a great job, you are more likely to get tips, which increase your income.

Nowadays, there are many car drivers who use an automatic car wash to clean their cars, but there's still money to be made as a car washer if you do it by hand. This is especially true in smaller cities, where many don't have access to automatic car washers. Alternatively, you can work in these places as a car wash attendant, where you don't have to wash the cars but are there to collect the money and do other smaller tasks when needed.

A quick search online will show you many other options when it comes to looking for part-time jobs; these are far from being the only ones out there. Try to search for things that interest you and that you know you will enjoy doing. Try job search platforms such as Indeed, Glassdoor, FlexJobs, LinkedIn, or Getwork to see who's looking.

Freelancing Jobs

There are a lot of different jobs you can do when it comes to freelancing, but before we get into them, freelancing requires you to take care of how you're going to get paid and to set your own prices. Besides that, because you are your own employer, you need to be far more organized in how you do things. For instance, you need to keep track of the things you need to do, such as tasks and responsibilities, that will help you become more successful at what you do. Freelancing jobs are the most flexible type of work you can find because you can literally work whenever you want or can. However, many of us, especially throughout our teenage years, are far from organized, but you don't have to worry because this is a skill that can be learned and will be very useful for you in the future. There are many tools that you can use, such as online calendars, other tracking apps, and to-do lists. For example, Google Calendar, TimeFree, and Timepage are excellent calendar apps. When it comes to tracking and to-do list applications, some of the best ones out there are Google Tasks, Things 3, or Todolist. Whatever you choose to use, what is important is that you keep everything in order so you know what tasks you should be doing.

Creating an online portfolio is crucial to bringing in clients, and this is not only for visual artists. These are important for any type of freelancing job, from writers to voice actors or transcriptionists. Your potential clients want to know what your level of skill is before hiring you, and this is the only way for them to know. You will also need to know how you're getting paid, and this is something that should be done before you accept your first job. While some jobs might pay directly to your bank account, this method of payment is not very common in freelancing. Usually, online services such as PayPal or Payoneer are far more common and secure to use. You also need to discuss this with the client beforehand to understand the best way for them to pay you. When it comes to actually getting paid, don't deliver any work until at least some of the payment has been transferred to you. The best way to do this and to ensure that no one gets scammed is by getting paid in two tranches: one before the start of the work and one at the end.

Becoming great at marketing is also important because you will find that there's quite some competition, so it's crucial that you understand your target market and spend some time creating your marketing plan. However, nowadays, it has become a lot easier to do this through social media platforms and your dedicated website.

Now, onto the most common freelancing jobs for you. Online tutoring is a great job if you're interested in pursuing any academic field and like to teach. Obviously, you need to teach grades below yours, or if you know a foreign language, you might find yourself getting a great income. Some of the most sought-after subjects are mathematics and science, such as physics or chemistry. When doing this type of work, you need to be extremely organized and have excellent communication skills. Of course, you don't have to be a master at it, but you need to want to learn and become better at it.

Digital artistry is also a job where you can earn a great income, but you need to have a particular skill and be interested in the genre. If you like to create anything through the digital medium, you can sell your art online. Alternatively, you can also work as a digital artist through an agency, but here, you're more likely to have to create art that clients require instead of creating your own and selling it. The requirements for this job differ depending on the type of digital art you want to create, but being good at drawing and understanding at least the basics of animation software can go a long way in this field.

Freelance writing is a job for those who are quite creative with written content, and it's perhaps one of the freelancing jobs where you have the most subgenres to choose from. You can become a ghostwriter, a social media writer, write commercial slogans, etc. There are many different types of writing to choose from. It requires you to have a great knowledge of the written word as well as grammar, and if you want to increase your income, you might want to specialize in a certain industry, such as finance or business.

A virtual assistant, often simply called VA, is a job where you work directly with clients and help them with their daily routine, such as answering emails, doing online research, or keeping track of their meetings and deadlines. Like freelance writing, you can work in many different industries and pick the one that interests you more. You have to be extremely organized since it's a big part of your job, but you also have to be proficient at working with a computer and have great communication skills.

Voice acting is not for everyone, but it's certainly a great job to do if you like it and can. Often, these jobs require you to record readings, such as from a book or other texts, or be a voice actor. However, you might need to purchase some equipment beforehand, such as a microphone or recording software, so you can record your material at home.

If you love video games, you can become a game tester, and it won't even feel like work! Basically, the job is to test new video games to find bugs, typos, or any other type of error before the game comes out to the public. Depending on the platform the games are on, you might have to have that specific platform to test the game, but the majority of these might be done on a computer. A great ability to write reports and good attention to detail are essential for these types of jobs.

Transcriptionists are a common job in the freelancing world, and it often consists of listening to a recording and writing it down. You might also have to proofread your written text or simplify the transcribed text. Much like freelance writing, you need to have a good grasp of the written language.

Regardless of what you want to do as a freelancer, creating accounts on some freelancing platforms is always a great idea, especially if you want to start building your portfolio. For instance, Upwork, 99Designs, ZipRecruiter, or Toptal are great places to start. Again, quick online searches will point you to many other reputable websites and sources on how you can get started.

Entrepreneurship Jobs

Perhaps you want to not only have control over your hours but also start your own business, grow it, and eventually do it full-time (or not). Coming up with your own business allows you to develop different types of skills that freelancing or working part-time doesn't, but you also have quite a few more responsibilities. Obviously, the first thing you have to do is choose what you want to do, such as the industry and the company you want to create.

One of the things many teenagers have, even when they might not have a lot of experience, is knowledge of technology and the online world. And this is certainly something that you can take advantage of since you probably understand the current trends and what people will be willing to use or buy. So, becoming an online marketer might be where your knowledge of the online world and entrepreneurship align. Couple your internet and online knowledge with your social media knowledge, and you can establish your own online marketing company.

Your creativity doesn't have to be bound to digital art; in fact, you can make it big through custom crafts if that's what you like to do. It's quite frequent to see teenagers and others selling things on Etsy; however, you don't have to only sell that, and you shouldn't if you want your business to grow. These crafts can be anything, really, from jewelry to decorations or anything in between, depending on what you want to do. The start is the hardest part, but you can do it by selling your crafts to family and friends and advertising them online.

If you want to run a business in a physical place (as opposed to being at home), something like being a snow cone shop owner might be interesting for you. This is actually one of the easiest ways to start your entrepreneurial career. There are a lot of things that you need to think about, such as what kind of storefront you'd like or what you want it to look like.

If you've washed cars before and want to continue in the same industry, perhaps automotive detailers are exactly what you are looking for. If you think that you don't have the necessary experience, you can start working in the detailing business in another company, but many, after getting the necessary experience, prefer to start their own mobile detailing company.

If you're really great with computers and you believe you have an excellent idea and know how to program, then starting your own tech business might be the single best thing you'll do. Many tech giants started this way, and you can even start working for other tech companies that accept teenagers, such as Vivint.

Obviously, these are just some ideas, and there are many other different things you could be doing. But one thing that I've learned is to first understand what you're good at and what you like to do, and then start from there to try and find what you are going to do.

How to Develop the Necessary Skills for Your Career Ahead?

There are many different skills you will have to learn that will have to do with your career and others that won't, but some of these that will help you progress in your career later in life are general and necessary.

For example, money and budgeting skills are essential, regardless of what career you might follow. Understanding how to make a budget and remain focused on it, how you can open a bank account, transfer money online, apply for a credit card, or write a check. Or how to maintain financial records, understand and assess basic market values, or how to save, purchase, or invest. We will go through this particular subject more in-depth later in the book.

Social skills and manners are also things that will probably help you in your career. This is how you are going to portray yourself in different social settings and will determine the impression you will have on others. Some of the things that might help you with that are learning how to make friendships and maintain them, exploring hobbies and interests, and meeting people with similar interests. Understand the value of the people in your life, and respect their views regardless of how against them you might be. Lastly, learning party etiquette, how to be a good guest, and how to host can help you meet new people and maintain those with whom you've formed a good relationship.

As I've mentioned, organizational skills will come in handy in any career you pursue, so learning as much as you can will make your life much easier. There's a great rule that I always like to mention called the rule of Kaizen, which essentially says "a place for everything and everything in its place." Besides that, there are other little things that you can do, such as declutter your space and reorganize so you know where everything is at any given time.

Communication skills are essential in any job where you have to communicate with others, which is practically all of them, at least to a certain extent. You have to get the message you want people to hear across as cleanly as you possibly can. There are many ways you can practice this, such as being aware every time you have to relay some information to someone on a daily basis. However, there are other things that you need to pay attention to, such as understanding who you are talking to. Everybody is different, and people have the most diverse temperaments, so you might have to communicate in a different manner. Being empathic and trying to understand the other person's perspective can also help you formulate the way you are speaking to them.

Behavioral skills are a way to show your character. Obviously, you build a strong personality, but you have to work on it, not simply wish for it. For instance, admitting your mistakes or taking responsibility for actions you've taken instead of hiding or blaming someone else. Apologizing when you're wrong is also important, and I understand that sometimes it is not an easy thing to do. Always being polite to anyone, regardless of who they are, or understanding the concept of morality so you can rightfully stand up for the things you believe in. Asking for help when you're in need can be a great thing to do. Many of us are too proud to ask for help, but often, that simply makes things worse.

You might also want to develop skills for coping with your emotions. We live in a stressful place where emotions often run high. Camping with these emotions can help you make better decisions or even strengthen ties with other people. For instance, chances are that when you go to college, you might experience loneliness if you leave your parents behind and go study in another city. Self-management allows you to be in control of what is going on in your head. This can be done in many different ways, but meditating or taking time for yourself to let those emotions run through you can help you get through those difficult times. It will also allow you to avoid making impulsive decisions that can have negative consequences.

You will face problems in your career that you will need to solve, and here, problem-solving skills will really come in handy. While your parents might have helped you solve some of your issues, you can't expect them to continue to do that once you grow up and start taking on more responsibilities. While you will get more experience the more problems you solve, this is really a self-learning skill. The first thing you have to do is start facing your problems and stop running away from them. Then, you have to identify the problem correctly so you can start looking for solutions. It's crucial that you analyze the different solutions you've come up with and understand the different outcomes. When you've gone through all of that, you can apply the solution with the best outcome.

Goal setting is essentially understanding how to prioritize the things you have to do. Understand where you want to go and come up with a plan to do it. Here, it's also important that you identify the resources that can help you achieve the goals you've set, and at times, you might even have to change or adjust your goals to suit your needs. The main thing here is to focus on the ultimate goal and devise a plan with smaller goals to get there.

Do you perhaps think that you don't have time to do everything you'd like to? While you might be very busy, there's a chance that your time management is not developed enough to carry out all the tasks you have. There are only 24 hours in which you can try and fit everything you have to do in, and having great time management skills can really help you do that. Using a calendar, a timetable, or even a planner where you can write down all the things you need to do throughout the day is a simple way to keep tabs on everything you have to do. You also have to become good at scheduling and sticking to the things you plan because if you take a little longer on certain things, your time might not be enough to go through everything. Here, it's also relevant that you learn how to prioritize certain tasks over others since some of the things that you might have scheduled might be more urgent or time-pressing. The most important thing, however, is to develop routines so it becomes easier for you to manage your time.

Lastly, another set of skills that will help you in your career are employability skills. These encompass some of the sets of skills I've already mentioned, such as communication, decision-making, and critical thinking. But others, such as work ethic, adaptability, leadership, or teamwork, will make you more likely to be employed in better positions.

As you can see, there are a myriad of jobs that you can take on, depending on what interests you. I've taken on my share of different jobs throughout my teenage years so I could have a solid base of different skills to work with in the future. Obviously, you don't have to work in every industry, but trying out different types of work, such as freelancing, part-time work, or entrepreneurship, might be helpful to learn skills that will stay with you for life. Besides that, you will also have to develop some other skills that you might learn by working and getting experience, but also by practicing them. These are crucial not only to increase your employment rate but also if you want to choose an entrepreneurial path to becoming a great boss.

A Few Words About Taxes

Taxes are mandatory payments to the government and are paid not only by individuals like you and me but also by businesses and corporations. These are used to fund government activities such as services or public works like schools or roads, but also to fund governmental organizations and other programs such as Social Security. Essentially, the taxes that we all pay serve as income for the government to pay for the most varied things. Income taxes are what most individuals pay, and they are automatically taken out of your monthly income, which you can see in your pay stub. But another common tax we pay is capital gains, which are taken out of any interest received from our investments, such as dividends. It's a crime to try and avoid taxes, and it's called tax evasion. However, there are certain things that an individual can do to alleviate the tax burden within the laws, and that's called tax avoidance. Governments use an agency to collect these taxes. For example, in the US, this is called the Internal Revenue Service, or IRS. What you pay in taxes is usually proportional to what you earn, so the more you earn, the more you pay.

While if you work for a company, you don't have to do anything to pay taxes since the company's account does everything for you, and the taxes are taken directly from your pay stub if you are self-employed, then you have to do your own taxes. There are many ways to do this, and many different third-party companies that can help you do this easily, such as TurboTax. However, if you think you can file it yourself, you can go to the IRS website and do it for free. This is for the US; of course, other countries have other entities that collect taxes. For instance, in the UK, it's HMRC. The process is the same; you can do it yourself, which takes some time, or you can find a company that simplifies the process for you. Every other country works more or less the same way; you just need to look for the entity that collects taxes in that specific country. If you need help on how to actually file the forms in the US, you can use the USA. gov website, where they tell you exactly what forms you have to file and how to do it. Every tax collector's website should also have a step-by-step guide on how to file the tax and fill out the form for that specific country.

In the next chapter, I will go through the financial part of things, such as how to open a bank account, what the different bank accounts are and their main functionalities, and many other things that will be useful for you to make the right decisions.

CHAPTER 3

BANKING AND FINANCIAL SERVICES

> *A big part of financial freedom is having your heart and mind free from worry about the what-ifs of life.*
>
> — *Suze Orman*

U nderstanding how the banking system works is fundamental to your money skills. There's no other way around it than to open a bank account and be able to manage it. It's actually quite easy, and many teenagers already have some sort of bank account opened by their parents. If you don't, it's alright; simply follow the steps I'll list below.

Opening Your First Bank Account

To open a bank account, first, you need to choose a bank to open with and give them some of your information. If you're under the age of 18, you might need your parents to open it for you, but you will still have access to it. However, there are also teen bank accounts, which are similar to other accounts with only a few features missing. For example, you can't have an overdraft or a credit card, and if you're over 16, you won't need a guardian or a parent to open it for you. Besides that, you can do everything you want with the account, such as setting up direct debits, making bank transfers, etc. However, to register a debit card yourself, you also need to be over 16 years old; otherwise, a parent or guardian will have to authorize it first.

Whether or not you need a parent or guardian to open an account, there's information that needs to be passed on to the bank, such as proof of address, contact information, and proof of identity, which can be a birth certificate, passport, or a driver's license if you already have one. If you have opened a teen bank account, once you turn 18 years old, it usually turns into an adult account right away so you can have all the features that were currently missing, but sometimes the bank provider might request that you authorize this change.

While I'll be talking about the different accounts you can apply for later in this chapter, when you're opening your first bank account, there are a few things that you need to take into account. For example, some bank providers have a minimum opening amount, which means that you need to add some money right away to the account when you open it. The amount differs, and it could be as little as $1, but you need to make sure what the minimum opening amount is before you apply for one. Another thing that you have to take into consideration is the monthly fee. While these often don't happen on teens' accounts, they might once you turn 18. Interest is also something worth checking because the money you have in your account grows depending on the interest rate; however, in regular checking accounts, there's usually no interest rate (we will talk more about this later on in the chapter). Some accounts (especially teen accounts) have limits such as withdrawals or spending limits, so you can't use more money if you reach a certain amount. While it might be a little annoying, it's a great way for you to learn how to handle and manage your money properly. Lastly, when thinking of opening a bank account, make sure it has a robust online banking app where you can track everything from your phone as well as make bank transfers. This makes things a lot easier.

The Different Types of Bank Accounts

There are a few different types of accounts that you can open; however, as a teenager, you can only open a checking account. Besides that, other bank accounts include savings, money market accounts (MMAs), and certificate of deposit accounts (CDs). Understanding the differences is crucial so you can make better decisions.

Checking Accounts

These types of accounts are the most basic ones and are essentially deposit accounts that you can first open. You can hold funds, transfer them, withdraw money at ATMs, or use paper checks. These can also be linked to other accounts (usually through the same bank institutions), such as savings accounts. Banking institutions have many different types of checking accounts, such as teen checking, student, senior, rewards, or interest (since the basic checking account doesn't have interest associated with it). But to start with, a basic checking account is fine as long as you understand the minimum deposit requirements (if any), the minimum balance requirements (if any), if there are monthly maintenance fees, if there are ATM fees, and the ATM network size (this allows you to know how many ATMs you can withdraw money from).

Setting up an account is easy. As a teen, you might need a parent or guardian to do it, but usually, you can do it online or by visiting a branch, and the process is usually immediate. Obviously, you will have to provide some important and personal information, such as an ID and Social Security number. Depositing cash can usually be done through a check or cash, and you will get a debit card linked to that account that you can use to pay for things or withdraw money. Like in many other accounts, your funds are protected up to $250,000 by the Federal Deposit Insurance Corporation or FDIC. This means that if there's any error by your bank or something happens to your money while it's in your bank account, you are covered as long as it's below the threshold. You can usually opt to have an overdraft or not in your account. I personally don't recommend it since this allows for debts where the fees are quite high. Besides allowing you to use an ATM and debit cards, other services used with a checking account include wire transfer, which is essentially moving money from one account to another electronically, or direct deposit, where, say, your employer pays your income directly into your account, which becomes immediately available to you.

Savings Account

The main difference between savings and checking accounts is that with savings, you have an interest rate, which means that for as long as you hold money in the account, the amount is increasing. In other words, the savings account pays you interest on the amount of the deposit you have in the account. All the things that you have to check when opening a checking account, such as the minimum balance, etc., are also relevant when you open a savings account. But while checking accounts usually allow you limitless withdrawals, savings accounts don't because they are not designed for everyday use. They also usually don't have a debit card, which is usually linked to your checking account, so any transfers are usually conducted from there.

These accounts are created to hold your money there and withdraw from it as little as possible because, as I've mentioned, the interest you earn is based on the money you have deposited there. The more money you have there, the more you earn in interest. But the most important thing to look for when opening a savings account is the annual percentage yield (APY), which is essentially the percentage you earn on the money deposited. The higher the APY, the more you earn. Every bank offers different percentages, and while you might think the higher, the better, these high-yield savings often have more conditions that you need to abide by, for instance, fewer withdrawals, withdrawals that take longer, or higher maintenance fees. If you want to have a savings account but don't want to have limited withdrawals, you can choose an easy-access savings account that allows you to withdraw money whenever you want, but these usually have a lower APY. It really all comes down to your needs. If you think you won't need the money, it's best to place it in a high-interest savings account; if not, it might be best to deposit it in a lower-interest account where you have easier access to your money.

There are other accounts that I will just briefly mention, such as a money market account (MMA) or a certificate of deposit account (CDs). MMAs can be seen as a mix of checking and savings accounts where you can deposit money in them, earn interest, have a debit card, and even have paper checks. However, with these accounts, you still have a withdrawal limit, but you can set up direct debits. Some of the main differences with these accounts include, for instance, a higher minimum balance requirement if you want to keep the account open. These are great when you want to earn interest but still want all the convenient features a checking account has to offer, such as the use of a debit card. CDs are time deposit accounts, which means that these mostly work as savings accounts where you leave your money there for a certain amount of time, which in the financial world is called "maturity term." During the maturity term, your money is increasing, or you're earning interest on the balance you have there.

When looking to open a bank account, it's also important that you not only look at the different brick-and-mortar bank providers but also at credit unions and online banks. Credit unions are customer-owned institutions that have many of the same services a big bank has and may even offer you better interest rates (although not always), mainly because they are non-profit organizations. Online banks often offer fewer fees because they don't have branches that they have to pay for, which means they might offer you better rates as well. However, because they don't have physical branches, all contact with the bank is done online through a computer or mobile phone.

To sum up the steps of opening a bank account, first, you need to choose how to apply (whether in branch, online, or through the phone), gather all the necessary information, such as your Social Security Number, ID, and proof of address, provide contact details, select the type of account you want, read and accept the terms and conditions, submit the application, and fund your account.

Managing Your Account

Usually, when you open any type of bank account, you will have to sign a document (usually the terms and conditions, which you have to read thoroughly). While sometimes you might have to sign and mail the documents, more often, you can sign the documents online before you can start using the account.

Checking and savings accounts need to be funded before you can start using them, which can be done in different ways, such as by depositing cash, depositing a check (which usually takes a couple of business days to reach your account), setting up a direct debit from your employer, which is nowadays the most common way to get your income, or transferring funds electronically from another bank account that you might already have.

After that, if you're expecting a debit card, this should arrive at your address in a couple of days. From then on, you can pay bills online, make remote check deposits, and even sign up for alerts on your phone or email when your balance is low or when you withdraw money. Apart from that, the only thing that you should keep an eye on is your balance to see if there are fees incurred or if you need a minimum balance on the account.

Using Online Baking

Online banking, also known as internet banking, allows you to do pretty much everything banking-related online as opposed to going to a banking branch, which might include deposits, payment of online bills, or transfers. Nowadays, every banking institution has online banking in one way or another, where you can access your account through the banking app or through your computer. This makes things a lot easier, especially if you're quite proficient with new technology, and it saves you plenty of time. It's also a lot more convenient because it allows you to make transactions or pay bills anywhere you are, simply from your phone or computer, and all you need is one of those devices connected to the internet. Some financial institutions even allow you to open savings accounts and other accounts linked to your main account online, as well as set up direct debits or report changes in your account.

This advance in technology allowed us to have online-exclusive banks, which offer much lower costs or free banking features and better gains in terms of interest. And even though they don't have branches or ATMs of their own, you are still able to withdraw money from your online bank accounts from any other bank ATMs, so there's little change for you here if you decide to go for an online-only bank.

Advantages and Disadvantages of Online Banking

As I've mentioned above, convenience is certainly the best advantage of online banking, and you can perform the most common things from the comfort of your home on your phone or laptop. Transactions are extremely efficient, can be done almost instantly, and can open and close accounts just as easily. Besides that, you also have a lot of options when it comes to the different types of accounts to open, from high- or low-interest savings accounts to fixed deposits, etc.

Monitoring your finances also became a lot easier since you don't have to go to the nearest ATM or branch to check your funds and can simply do it anywhere on any device. Because of this, you have access to your account 24/7, which wasn't always the case when you had to wait for bank branches to open in the morning.

While I believe online banking makes banking accessible for everyone, including people who are just starting out in the financial world, it also comes with some disadvantages that you need to be aware of. In this case, the disadvantages I'll be listing target online-only banking institutions. For instance, if you are a new banking customer, not having someone to talk to face-to-face might be a little daunting at first, and customer service is only available over the phone or through chat. Online banking depends entirely on access to the internet, and if for any reason you don't have it, you become quite limited. Lastly, while online banking security is constantly improving, accounts are still subjected to hacking, but this refers to any type of online banking, even those belonging to brick-and-mortar banks.

Staying Safe With Online Banking

As I've said, online banking security is constantly improving, and it's quite secure, but it's still susceptible to hacking and other scams if you don't pay attention. There are a few things that you can do to make your accounts more secure and prevent your information from falling into a hacker's hands. One of the easiest things you can do is choose a strong password, as you'd normally do with any other online account. You can also enable two-factor authentication or, if you're on your phone, face identification, which allows you to only access the banking app after your face is scanned.

Alternatively, you can also sign up for banking alerts, so if there are any strange movements in your account, you will be notified right away, and you can then contact your bank to know more or to freeze your account. Steering away from public Wi-Fi connections is also a good way to prevent your information from spreading to other people. Use only private or well-secured Wi-Fi connections. Hackers can get your information through malicious hotspots, through malware and spyware on the Wi-Fi, or through data transmissions over unencrypted networks.

Other than that, simply pay attention to any phishing scams so you don't give your personal information away. There are many different ways these scams operate, but they all have the same finality: you giving your information away. This can be in the form of SMS texts or emails that usually look like they come from your bank. However, they often urge you to insert personal information on the website or to change your information and then redirect you to a website that often looks like your bank. Paying attention to the sender's email address is important, and you can check if that's actually your bank's email address. Alternatively, you can call your bank and ask them if they've sent an email from that email address. Hovering over the links on an email sent to you often allows you to see the webpage it is addressing you to. And lastly, your bank almost never asks you to share your personal information. When in doubt, contact your bank to make sure before you share any personal information.

Understanding Bank Cards, ATMs, and Fees

There's quite a lot more to know when it comes to all these financial services and products than you might think. Things like debit and credit cards might sound and look like the same thing, but they can be very different. The same goes for all the different fees these services and products might charge. So, let's go through all the most important things you need to know to use them with confidence.

Credit Cards vs. Debit Cards

When you look at both a debit and a credit card, there's not much difference, right? They have 16-digit numbers on them, as well as expiration dates, magnetic strips, etc. You can use both in the same way and use them to purchase things, but this is where things get a little different. When making purchases, a debit card draws money that you have in your bank account, while credit cards draw borrowed money from your bank and have a limit. So, in other words, a debit card uses your money, and a credit card uses the bank's money that you will need to pay back eventually. This is not to say that credit cards are bad; they are not. The way you use it might have negative implications for your finances. A credit card offers you security, but you need to know how to use it. Let's get down to it.

Credit Cards

As I've mentioned, a credit card is usually issued by a financial institution where you already have an account. The institution allows you to borrow money from them with the condition that you pay them back with interest, so you will always pay them back more than what you've spent. However, there are many different types of credit cards that might offer you different perks.

Regular credit cards are easy to understand, allow you to pay with borrowed money, make balance transfers, and are usually free (meaning no annual fees). Premium credit cards often have perks for their customers, such as access to special events, airport lounge access, and other things, but they incur an annual fee. Then, there are the specific rewards credit cards that give you travel points, which give you discounted airline tickets, cash back, and other rewards. Balance transfer credit cards usually have extremely low-interest rates as well as low fees from another credit card's balance transfer. Secured credit cards are for those people who can't get standard or any other type of credit card, and they have to pay an initial deposit as collateral to be able to use a credit card. Lastly, there are charge credit cards that do not have a limit, but usually, you'd have to pay the balance within a month before you could use them again.

There are quite a few benefits to using a credit card besides the security and rewards it gives you. For example, they help you build your credit history, which appears on your credit reports. Credit reports are important documents that allow banks and other financial institutions to check if you're financially trustworthy when you're asking for loans or a mortgage for your property. Credit cards help you build a stronger credit report because they show if you have been paying your credit card back on time, for instance. If you use your credit card properly, you can raise your credit score, get higher chances of getting accepted for loans, and get lower interest rates on those loans.

Most credit cards also allow purchase protections and warranties on items that you purchase, besides whatever retail warranty the company producing the item gives you. For instance, if you buy a TV with your credit card, you usually have a warranty that lasts a year or two, but if the TV stops working after the retail company's warranty, you can check if your credit card offers an extended warranty and has you covered. Some credit cards might also offer price protection, which allows you to replace any item that might have been lost or stolen or even get a refund.

Credit cards also have fraud protection in case of theft or loss, and if you report it in a timely manner, this is not exclusive to credit cards and debit cards. The Electronic Fund Transfer Act can give you the same protection, but again, you have to report it within 48 hours of finding out you've lost your card. But with a credit card, you are far more protected. For example, you can dispute an unauthorized purchase if the goods are lost during shipping or are delivered damaged under the Fair Credit Billing Act. If you have bought goods that have been lost or damaged during shipping with a debit card, you can only get a refund if the merchant wants it. Another example of credit cards being more secure is if you were to rent a car. Many credit card providers (but not all) allow a waiver for any collisions you might have.

But of course, there are cons when it comes to using credit cards, and you've probably heard some of them. For instance, the unhealthy use of credit cards can lead to large debts. As I've mentioned, when you're using a credit card, you're not using your money but the bank's money, which you will have to pay back with interest at some point. You have to at least pay the minimum payment every single month, but the more you spend, the harder it becomes to pay at least those minimum payments. Plus, you should only pay the absolute minimum if you can't pay more because if you keep on paying the minimum, you will never finish paying your debt because of the rise in interest rates.

If you fail to make the minimum payments, that will have a negative impact on your credit score, but keeping the balance on your credit card at a low level will help your credit score. But if you do the opposite and fail to make credit card payments, max out your credit cards, or apply for too many credit cards, you will see your credit score decrease.

You can think of a credit card as a short-term loan, and these can get really high-interest rates, which are calculated using your annual percentage rate (APR). The higher the interest and APR, the more you pay in interest when you're paying back the money you've spent with your credit card. Also, keep in mind that the higher the interest, the harder it is for you to pay and the more it will cost you to pay what you owe. Besides the interest on your credit card, there are other fees that might also be applied and that you have to be aware of, such as a late payment fee, a cash advance fee, an annual fee (but not always), a balance transfer fee, or a foreign transaction fee. We will go deeper into credit later in its own dedicated chapter.

Debit Cards

As I've mentioned above, when you're paying with a debit card, you are not using anyone else's money but your own, which comes straight from your checking or savings account. With a debit card, you can only use as much money as you have deposited in the account. Like credit cards, debit cards can also offer some consumer protections, but credit cards usually offer more when it comes to fraud. While most debit cards are linked to a bank account, this is not strictly necessary. In fact, there are two types of debit cards that don't require you to have a savings or checking account: Prepaid debit cards and electronic benefits transfer (EBT) cards. The first is used by people who don't have a bank account but want to make electronic purchases and be able to use all the features a debit card allows. However, as the name indicates, you'd have to preload your card with the amount of money you'd like to have on it. So, for instance, if you wanted to have $300 in the prepaid debit card, you'd have to transfer that money first, and you cannot use more than what you've deposited. EBTs are issued by federal and state agencies, but only qualifying people can use them and have the benefits that come with them. Such benefits can include, for instance, food stamps or cash. Because these are essentially debit cards with a PIN number and a magnetic strip, they can be used in ATM machines and other point-of-sale terminals. The way it works is that once the recipient gets accepted or approved for benefits, the state they are in creates an account, and the Supplemental Nutrition Assistance Program (SNAP) benefits are placed in the account for them to use every month. By federal law, there are no processing fees or sales taxes on these purchases. These systems exist in the US, but other countries have their own that often work similarly.

When you use a debit card, you don't have the issue of incurring debt since all the money you spend with it is yours, and you don't have to pay it back to anyone. And it is known that people tend to spend more money when using a card (debit or credit) than when using cash, so if you use a debit card, you don't have the issue of racking up large debts. While credit cards still offer better fraud protection, debit cards are becoming better and better when it comes to this subject, and so they have become quite safe. As I've said, the quicker you report the missing card or any unusual activity, the better chances you have of getting the money back. There's also no annual fee on debit cards, unlike many credit cards. You also don't have a withdrawal fee with a debit card, which you do with a credit card.

Now, when it comes to the disadvantages of debit cards, they are not free from some. For instance, there are no rewards, with the exception of rewards checking accounts, but these are not as good as the perks from credit cards. Debit cards don't help you build credit like credit cards do. Essentially, when you pay back your credit card, you are telling lenders that you are financially trustworthy and that you will pay your money back. With a debit card, you don't have to pay it back, so you're not proving that you can be financially trustworthy. Lastly, even though debit cards don't have annual fees like credit cards do, you might have to pay other fees such as maintenance fees, overdraft fees, or even foreign ATM fees.

So, while credit and debit cards might look similar, their advantages and disadvantages are quite different. You need to understand your priorities when thinking about using one or the other. While it's recommended that you have both before you make a purchase, you need to understand if you want to start building your credit or getting rewards or if you prefer to have your finances totally under control. Obviously, using a bit of both might be the wisest thing you'd do, but when using your credit card, make sure you have enough money to pay your debt.

How Do You Use an ATM?

You probably know what an ATM is, and even if you've never used one before, you know it's a machine that allows you to withdraw money from your bank account. Out of curiosity, do you know what ATM stands for? I didn't for a long time after I started using it, but it stands for Automated Teller Machine, and it has many more different uses than simply withdrawing money from your bank account. It also allows you to make basic transactions without having to go to a bank and talk to a teller (hence the automatic teller). While most people use a debit card when withdrawing money, you can also use a credit card, although these usually come with a higher fee. ATMs are spread across the country and other countries and make it easier for you to use financial systems anywhere, which makes them quite convenient even nowadays, where financial services are dominated by the internet and mobile banking.

When it comes to fees, these are usually charged by the ATM operator, your bank, or both; however, if you use an ATM that is operated by your bank, these fees can be avoided. If you use an ATM in a foreign country, you are always likely to pay fees, even if they are only exchange rates.

There are two main types of ATM machines, with the most basic of the models only allowing you to check your account's balance and withdraw money. These are the most common ones seen anywhere. But there is another type that is often inside bank branches, and you hardly see them on a high street, for instance. These allow you to perform more services such as transfers, access account information, accept deposits (often cash), and aid you with a line of credit payments. Obviously, you have to have an account at that same bank to be able to use these more complex ATM machines.

Apart from that, the common design of ATM machines is pretty straightforward. There's a card reader where you insert your card, so the ATM knows your bank details. The keypad allows you to enter your PIN or the amount you want to withdraw or send; there's also a cash dispenser from where the ATM "gives" you the money. ATMs also have a printer in case you want to have a copy of the receipt of whatever service you've just performed, and of course, a screen where you can see what is happening and allow you to guide yourself through the process.

When it comes to using it, it's also quite simple. You will have to insert your bank card, and it will prompt you to type your PIN. From there, you will see on the screen some options, such as withdrawing money or checking your balance. As I've mentioned, if you don't want to be charged for any transactions, you should use the ATM operated by your bank since ATMs operated by other banks or other ATM operators will incur a fee upon transaction. This is especially important if you withdraw money quite often, which might add up at the end of the week or month. There's usually a certain amount that you can withdraw per day, week, or month, but these differ depending on your bank and bank account. While some might limit your daily withdrawal to $300, others might allow a $1500 daily withdrawal. However, if you need to withdraw more than the limit, you can usually get around this by calling your bank and asking for permission, or you can go directly to a branch and talk to a teller.

Opening your first bank account is quite exciting since it will allow you to have a little more financial freedom. It's important that you shop around and check out the best banks for your first account. This should align with the purpose of your bank account—what are you using it for, etc.? Then, you have to choose your account type, and the first one is almost always a regular checking account. In fact, you can't open a savings account without opening a checking account first. Then you have MMAs and CDs, but these can come later. Because you might be tech-savvy, you will have a much easier time managing your account through your phone via mobile or internet banking. The advance of this technology allows us to simplify how people manage their accounts, which has become fairly easy. Lastly, understanding the differences between credit and debit cards is crucial so you don't end up accumulating a lot of debt. To start with, chances are you won't need a credit card, and if you're working part-time, as a freelancer, or even as an entrepreneur but still living with your parents, I don't think you will need a credit card. However, if you do take one, make sure you understand the terms and conditions, the APR, and everything else that is involved when it comes to spending money with a credit card.

In the next chapter, I will talk about budgeting, which is oftentimes linked to your capacity to spend only the money that you have (as opposed to using credit cards). Here, I'll introduce the concept of budgeting, why it's so important, how you can create your own personal budget by tracking your income and expenses, how you can allocate funds to the different categories, how you can manage irregular income (if you're a freelancer or an entrepreneur), and talk about some of the most common strategies when it comes to budgeting.

CHAPTER 4

BUDGETING

> *A budget is more than just a series of numbers*
> *on a page; it is an embodiment of our values.*
>
> — *Barack Obama*

Budgeting is the only way we can understand if we are on the right path in terms of finances. Sure, you've heard of a budget and budgeting before, and you might even have a faint idea of what it is exactly. But having a budget is one of the most fundamental things we can do to understand how our finances work and how to be successful when it comes to money. Essentially, with a budget, you can tell where the money is coming from and where it's going, and that's the only way to get absolute control of your money. Now, if we want to get a little more technical, a budget allows you to track your income and expenses and establish a balance of what you can and can't spend throughout a month (or more).

There are several ways to create a budget with more or fewer variants, but a budget always has to have three fundamental things: it has to have an identity, which in this case is you (although there are also budgets for companies, governments, households, etc.). There has to be a defined time period, for instance, a month (businesses tend to do longer budgets). And it has to have detailed information on where the money is coming in (such as from your employer or freelancing work) and where the money is going (where you spend the money, etc.).

Let me give you an example of what the personal budget of a teenager might look like. Say you started working part-time on the weekends, and you're earning $500 a month. Because you are still living with your parents, you are not paying rent, bills, etc. But instead, you're saving a part of it, and the rest is for expenses such as a night out every week and traveling to work on the weekends. Everything else goes to savings.

	Income		Expenditures
Salary	$500	Night outs	$200
		Traveling	$20
Total (savings):	$280		

This is a pretty easy budget since you don't have to pay for groceries, bills, etc., but once you start doing that, things get a little more complex and you will need to allocate certain amounts to certain places and not exceed them. For instance, if you wanted to save $380 instead of $280, you'd have to cut your nights out in half.

Why Should You Care About Budgeting?

Well, if I haven't convinced you yet about starting to budget, I can come up with a few more reasons as to why you should be budgeting, especially if you want to save as much as possible. First of all, starting to budget at a young age will teach you the basics of money habits and mindset that we've discussed in the previous chapter. This alone should be reason enough to convince you, but there's more.

Budgeting allows you to set and reach your long-term goals, regardless of what they are. For instance, there's this trip that your friends are planning to do, and, obviously, you want to go with them, but while you have money for the flight, you don't have enough for the accommodation. Because the trip is a year away, you might still have time to save some money to go, but I know that when you're a teenager, one year is very far away. Either way, the logic is the same. The accommodation is $1000 for five days, and using the example from above, you are saving $280 a month. This means that in about four months, you'll be able to pay for the accommodation. However, your friends are only willing to wait three months for you to book the accommodation because they say that particular place gets full rather quickly. So, you have to go back to your budget and relocate some of the money so you can save more. Looking at it, the only thing that you can really change is the nights out because you need to pay for travel if you want to continue to have an income. So, if you cut the money you spend on your night outs in half, you'd have $380 saved a month. This means that in three months, you'd have enough time to book the accommodation. Without a budget, you wouldn't know exactly where you'd have to cut and how much you could spend on certain things. It essentially forces you to plan your goals and to know exactly how much you can spend and how much you need to allocate to the different expenses and savings. You have a great overview of money coming in and money coming out, which allows you to know how much you have progressed and how far your goal is.

Budgeting can keep you from overspending, especially on money that you don't necessarily have. Assuming you have a credit card, overspending can become a really bad situation because you are spending money that is not yours, you have to pay it back, and you don't have that money. With a budget, you know exactly how much you can spend and when you should stop. As a teenager, this is easier to understand because you have fewer expenses and, most likely, don't have a credit card yet. However, this will change in the future, and you have to be prepared to plan a budget and stick to it. Before, when people used cash instead of cards, things were also simpler because the fact that you visualized money coming out of your wallet made you think about it. Nowadays, you don't see that money, and so it's easy to simply type a PIN or even touch your card (with contactless payments), and that's it; you don't think about it anymore. This is also one of the reasons budgeting is important: it can keep you in line and make sure you don't spend without thinking.

Budgeting can make your retirement savings a lot easier. I know that retirement is a long way from where you are now, and we will talk about it later in the book. But once you get there and have been budgeting all those years, you will be thankful you've done it. Budgeting doesn't only make retirement savings easier, but all savings in general. It's crucial that you build regular savings and make contributions to your retirement accounts so you don't have to worry about not having enough once you retire.

I've briefly mentioned emergency funds, which are quite necessary if, well, an emergency appears. Budgeting allows you to save, which means that it also allows you to build a financial cushion in case of an emergency. Obviously, as a teen, you might have your back covered by your parents, but as soon as you start your young adult life, you might be on your own, so you will want to save as much as you can to start your adult life and have no issues navigating it.

Budgeting can also reveal your spending habits. For instance, if we use the example above, you know you'd be spending $200 a month on nights out. That's a big chunk of your income. However, when you start your young adult life, you will have far more expenses. Things like TV or streaming subscriptions might add up and take a big chunk of your income. Without a budget, you might not even notice any of that. Only once you list all your expenses do you start to understand how much you usually spend on things that you probably shouldn't. Not only that, but it might also reveal bad spending habits such as purchasing too many clothes, unnecessary food, etc., that you might be able to stop.

How Should You Create a Personal Budget?

While budgets can be created in different ways and also depend on each person's lifestyle, there are a few steps that you can follow to make this right. The small changes you will be able to figure out as you gain more experience creating budgets.

The first step is to create your net income. This might be a new word for you, but it simply means your take-home income. So, if you're only working part-time, you probably are not paying any taxes yet. But once you move to a full-time job, some expenses, such as taxes and retirement programs, will be deducted from your pay. Usually, you don't have to worry about it, and the accountant of your employer does that. The important aspect here is finding out how much you're actually making or how much is entering your account each month. Calculating your income gets a little harder if you have an irregular income, for instance, if you are a freelancer or an entrepreneur; however, you can write down and find out how much you're making.

The next step is tracking your spending, and this is where you might find some revelations about your spending habits. First, you should list your regular spending, such as bills, mortgage, rent, etc. In the example I've used, your regular spending would be your traveling (and not your night outs!). Other things, such as utilities or car payments, are also part of your regular payments. Then, you have to list your variable expenses, and these are a little harder to find out because, well, they are irregular. Your night outs would fall into this category because even though you might spend more or less the same every time you go out, there might be times when you spend a little less or a little more. Other variable expenses would be groceries or gas. This is also the best area where you can reduce your overall expenses because most of them might not be necessary (yes, night outs are not as necessary as paying your rent). But obviously, fixed expenses can also be cut; for example, you could change your phone provider if you think you're paying too much or your energy provider. To help you find all of this information, credit and debit card statements are your best resources because you will have a detailed list of where your money came from and where it went.

When doing your budget, you need to set goals, but it's important that these goals are realistic. Before you even analyze all the information you've tracked, you should write down a list of your goals: short-, medium-, and long-term goals. In the short-term goals, things like setting up an emergency fund should be listed, as well as any other short-term goal you want to achieve, such as going on a trip with your friends. Long-term goals should be things that will take some time to achieve, such as saving for a down payment on a property or retirement. Of course, these goals can change over time, which will change the way you set up your budget, but what's important is that you have them so you can keep yourself motivated.

When that's done, it's time to make a plan. This is where you take all the information you've gathered and bring everything together. The first thing is to look at what you're actually spending and compare it with what you actually want to spend. When you have those side by side, then you have to start looking for ways to cut down on some of the expenses. It's easier to cut down on variable costs such as going out, TV or streaming subscriptions, etc.

Again, you have to do your budgeting at least every month because it will need constant adjustments. But you also have to adjust your spending so it stays within your budget. Once you've followed all the steps until now, you'll have a much clearer idea of the things you need to adjust and where you can't overspend. Here, I like to make two columns of my expenses, one with my wants and another with my needs. The first thing that you can cut is anything in the "wants" column. For instance, do you really need to go to the movies once a week? Or can you have movie nights at home? Either way, movie night is not a need; it's a want. Food, rent, mortgage, transport, etc. Those are needs, and even for those, you might find a solution on how to decrease spending. The main thing to take from here is that even small decreases and changes can add up at the end of the month.

The last step is to regularly check on your budget, ideally every month because expenses and even income might change. The hard part is starting, but once you have a budget, you can simply adjust it every month. This is a habit that you should try to incorporate into your routine, and you will see the difference that will make.

Budget Allocation

While right now you might not have as many sections in your budget as you will once you have your independence, it's important that you understand what budget allocation is. There are many different categories that you can make when setting up your allocation, which might be a little daunting, but there are a few that should always be incorporated. It all comes down to how much more control you want over your money, your spending habits, and your goals. All of this will allow you to organize your money and reach your financial goals faster.

When you're just starting to budget, I find it easier to first catalog the different sections as "essential" and "non-essential." As we've discussed, essential spending has to do with the things that you have to spend money on regardless, such as rent or mortgage, groceries, travel, etc. Non-essential is everything else that doesn't fall into the first category.

There's a very popular budget rule called the 50/30/20 rule, where you allocate 50% of your income to your needs (essential), 30% to your wants (non-essential), and 20% to savings. Of course, this is just a guide, and you might have to adjust it. Also, there are many other budgeting strategies that I will talk about later in this chapter. Now, once you get independence, there will be many other categories in your budget, and I like to divide it into five different categories: Housing that encompasses rent or mortgage; transportation that involves public transportation tickets, gas, car maintenance, car loan payment, etc.; utilities such as electricity, water, mobile, internet, and cable; food and supplies, such as groceries, household items, cleaning supplies, and savings. These categories might expand if or when you have a child or a pet, or both, in which case you'd add another category, childcare, where you'd insert babysitting, nursery, and daycare, and a pets category, where you'd add pet food, vet bills, flea treatments, toys, etc.

This is quite a basic budget category, but obviously, there are other things that you will need to add as you get better at budgeting, such as healthcare, insurance, personal care, or clothing. You can add more categories as you see fit for your lifestyle, as these are just simple ideas.

Now, you might be asking, "How much money should I be allocating to the different categories?" Well, that depends on your needs. I've already given you an example with the 50/30/20 method, but it really depends. One thing is certain: your needs have to be met, and that's a great way to start your budget. But the different categories you add simply have to work for you. After all, it is a personal budget and a personal process. Everybody has a different income, different expenses, needs, and goals, and it's hard to give the right number.

What If I Have an Irregular Income?

If you have an irregular income, then things get a little more complicated, but nothing that you can't overcome. Here, you need a different approach. You might not know your income for sure, but you know your expenses, at least the fixed ones. This is where I would start when budgeting on an irregular income. For instance, you'd still have rent or a mortgage, bills, groceries, and maybe travel costs. While these can also vary, they are easier to predict. When you've written down the fixed expenses, you need to make sure that you can at least cover them every month.

Another thing that you can do is budget for the lowest monthly income you can have. It might be tempting to budget for a good month when your income is irregular, but you should budget for your lowest income so you know for sure you can make it. Here, it's also important that you think ahead since different months and seasons could mean more or less income. This is especially true if you're self-employed. There are certain industries where certain seasons, such as Summer or Christmas, might bring in more money while others might bring in less. You should try to save more during the higher income periods so you can then pay for those months when business is less stable.

Different Budgeting Strategies

As I've said before, there are many different budgets, but they simply serve as a template from which you have to make your own adjustments so they fit your lifestyle. In any case, I'll show you some of the most popular budgeting strategies used in personal finance so you can have a better idea of where to start.

Again, I like to emphasize that when you start budgeting, it might be hard to stay on track, and that's one of the reasons you should start now when you have fewer expenses so you can create the habit. But let's get to the strategies.

I've already mentioned the 50/30/20 formula, sometimes known as the balanced money formula, but I want to explain some of its benefits. This is an easy budget to start with because it only has three simple categories, which means less calculation and fewer worries. However, overspending can happen when using this strategy because there's more leeway, and it's not as strict. This comes from the fact that you are not budgeting for every category, like food or gas, which might mean that if you don't pay attention, you might overspend. If you follow this budget, I recommend that you overestimate a little so you have some room for overspending.

Cash-Only Budget

This strategy is exactly as the name indicates: You only use cash (if you still remember what cash is, of course). This strategy is also called envelope budgeting because you place the cash in different envelopes, and on each one of those envelopes is written the purpose of that money. This means you wouldn't be using your bank cards. Nowadays, using this method is not as easy as it once was because most things we pay are standing orders, but there are certain categories where you can only use cash. For example, you can add $200 to an envelope named "groceries." So, you would withdraw $200, write "groceries" on an envelope, and place that cash on that envelope. That's all you can spend on groceries. Once that money is gone, you can't purchase more. You can also do this for gas, clothing, etc.

This is a great strategy if you overspend often. It's quite simple: once there's no more cash in that specific envelope, you can't spend more. To make this method more efficient, make sure you leave your bank cards at home. One thing that you should pay attention to when using this budgeting method is to be extra careful since you're using cash and can lose it. Make sure all the money you carry is in a safe place.

Zero-Based Budget

The zero-based budget, which many refer to as the budget where you "give every dollar a job," is exactly that. Every income money has a purpose, meaning that your income matches every money outgoing from your account. Obviously, this doesn't mean you spend all your money, but instead, at the end of the month, you shouldn't have any money in your checking account because you've also transferred some to an external savings account. Essentially, all your money has a purpose, and you shouldn't have money in your regular checking account because it's not bringing you any benefits.

Some of your income has the job of paying the bills, paying rent or mortgage, while another portion goes for savings, groceries, etc. You should use this budget technique if you want absolute control of your money, where you essentially micromanage everything. In other words, you wouldn't spend any money unless it had been planned before. However, this is quite a time-consuming budget because it involves a lot of planning, and you'd be recording every single transaction. So, while it gives you total control over your income, you need to have time to actually make it work.

The 60% Solution Budget

This budget strategy is in many ways similar to the zero-budget one in the sense that you use every single dollar of your income somewhere. Essentially, 60% of your income goes to committed expenses, and this includes both fixed and non-fixed expenses, so you can have a mortgage or rent, but also gas, cable, streaming services, etc. In other words, every expense that comes every month falls into this 60%. The rest (40%) is then divided into four 10% groups, such as long-term savings, short-term savings, retirement, and wants. Long-term savings include emergency funds and any investments you might want to make. Short-term savings is any goal that you want to save up for that is coming soon, such as vacations. The retirement allocation is the money that goes to retirement accounts such as 401(k)s (which I will discuss later in the "Retirement" chapter). If these are done through your employer, then you don't have to do them. Then, the want is anything that you want to do with the remaining 10%, such as going out for dinner, going to the cinema, etc.

This is a less intensive budget to follow while still using every dollar of your income for something. The issue with this method is that you might lean on percentages quite a lot and forget to track your expenses. You should still track everything so that you know that you're on the right path. Another thing to take into consideration is whether you're in a good financial position to actually follow this budget since not everybody is.

Value-Based Budget

This budget strategy works best if your income is high, so if you don't think you're in the higher-income bracket, this budget strategy is not for you. Also, this budget requires you to actively think about yourself and the things you want to do. In sum, this budget allows you to spend money on things that you give value to (which you still have to track) instead of making sure a certain percentage of your income goes towards a certain allocation. Here, you have to write down the things that you value most. So, for instance, if you value going out for dinner or traveling, that's what you should be writing down. Anything else that is not on your list, you shouldn't be spending money on.

This budget is also better suited for those who have some level of discipline and already have some savings. It also saves you more time since you're not trying to track every single dollar of your income.

If you don't have the discipline, this strategy is not for you because chances are that you will get off track easily. If you tend to spend money on things that are not really of any value to you, then this is also not for you. But this soul-searching when writing about the things that you value can be a way to really understand the things you like. For instance, you might think that you like to go watch an NBA game every month or so, but after some thinking about it, there might be many other things that you value more, so you don't add NBA games to your list.

Again, these are just guidelines that will help you come up with your own budget that will suit your needs. The most important thing is feeling comfortable with the budget you are creating every month. And don't forget that your income changes, as do your priorities, so make sure you adjust your budget accordingly.

Budgeting is a crucial thing to do when we are handling money. Without a good budget, you simply can't save enough money for the things you want to do and for your future. For this, you need to analyze how you spend your money and what your income is. Once you know exactly how these things work, you need to be able to properly allocate your income to things that matter to you, and that will help you reach your goals. However, budgeting is not an easy thing to do, and that is why it is so important to start now so you can create healthy habits that you will bring with you into adulthood. It is also not something that you do once; it needs to be constantly changing and adapting to fit your needs and your lifestyle, but it needs to be done.

The next chapter is like a continuation of this, where I will be talking about your spending and paying the bills. I'll dive into how you can make informed purchasing decisions, how you can differentiate between needs and wants, how to practice smart shopping, such as comparing prices, and other tips on saving money on bills.

CHAPTER 5

SPENDING AND PAYING BILLS

> *Do not save what is left after spending, but spend what is left after saving.*
>
> — *Warren Buffet*

Once you reach adulthood and independence, you will find that you have more freedom when it comes to the things you want to purchase. However, if you have not developed control over your finances as a teenager, in the form of budgeting, for instance, you will have a much harder time making the right financial decisions. This will then have consequences for your overall spending and needs, such as paying bills, etc.

There are other things that during your teenage years you can develop and become better at, such as differentiating between your needs and your wants, how to practice smart shopping and using other techniques such as comparing prices, and many other things I'll talk about in this chapter.

How Can You Make Informed Purchasing Decisions?

As the name indicates, to make better buying decisions, you need to be informed. So, the key here is to understand what you're buying so you can choose the best product or service over others.

The first thing you should do is ask yourself some questions. For instance, "If I buy this, how will it improve my life?" or "Do I really need this?" If whatever you're buying does improve your life significantly and you do need it, then you can ask, "Is a purchase the right thing to do? Couldn't I borrow it instead?" This often happens when what you are buying might be important and essential, but it's something that will only be essential once. And so, it begs the question, "How often will I use it?"

If it will make your life better, you cannot borrow it, and you might use it more than once; the questions don't end here. You should ask yourself, "Is now the best time to buy it?" These are the types of questions you should ask yourself before any purchase you make so you can determine if you should make one or not.

You also need to consider your current savings, especially if it's an expensive thing. Imagine that you need that, but it's quite expensive, and you don't have the savings for it. Is it worth it to take out a loan for it? Is this a planned purchase? If this is planned and you have savings, then by all means; however, if it was planned and you don't have the savings, perhaps you might consider holding off on the purchase until you can afford it. Taking out a loan to purchase something should be your last resort, especially if what you're purchasing won't bring you any income.

What I like to do when facing some purchases is look at the cost-per-use. Here, you will be calculating the value of the good or service you are thinking of purchasing, and with that, you will have more information about the potential purchase. It is also quite simple to calculate; all you have to do is divide the total cost of the item or service by the estimated number of times you will use it. You also have to think about the benefits of what you're buying. Here, you have to consider all its advantages and disadvantages. Will it bring in more money? Will it boost your productivity? If you purchase a new computer and work from home, perhaps in the long run, it will bring you some advantages, such as performing jobs quicker. If you invest in solar panels, in the long run, they will save you more money. On the other hand, purchasing a car is almost always a necessity if you live in an area where there's no public transport or it takes too long to get you where you want to be. This is because a car decreases in value from the moment you purchase it, plus you have to pay for maintenance, gas, insurance, etc. So, unless a car is the only way you can get to work and make some income, it is usually a bad investment.

Needs vs. Wants

I think one of the hardest things to do when you get financial independence is to distinguish between needs and wants, which is the basis for creating a good budget and making the right financial decisions. This is something that you have to do yourself. Of course, there are basic needs that we all have to prioritize, and I've mentioned most of them, such as rent or mortgage, groceries, or utility bills. Essentially, there are basic requirements that you must fulfill to live properly. They are things that you must have; they tend to remain constant over time, and their non-fulfillment can have serious consequences. Wants, especially in this context, can be described as services and goods that you might like to have, but they don't represent a necessity like needs do and are often a desire that is non-essential for you to live. They tend to change over time, unlike needs, and the non-fulfillment of these does not result in any tragedy, but it might result in disappointment for some time.

If you want to get a little more technical about needs and wants, I will give you another definition. Needs are requirements that are necessary for you to live and survive. If we go back to ancient times, humans had three needs: food, shelter, and clothing. But as time went on, our needs increased to encompass healthcare and education, not so much to survive as to improve our lives.

Wants, from an economic point of view, are things that you might wish to possess, often now but also at some point in the future. Most goods and services stem from wants and not needs, and that's one of the reasons many businesses are extremely wealthy because people really crave their wants. For instance, why would you want to buy the iPhone 14 when you bought the iPhone 13 last year? Your current iPhone 13 still works perfectly fine, but your desire to have that, for various reasons, will make you buy the new iPhone. This lack of control over our wants can really have a negative impact on our finances, and that's why it is so important to understand the difference between these two definitions and develop control over our wants.

How Can You Shop Smart?

While fixed expenses are hard to modify, you can save some money by reducing the price you pay for variable expenses, and this often comes in the form of smart shopping. There are many different ways you can reduce the cost of things, and I'm going to give you some ideas on how you can do that. While you might use many of these throughout your adulthood, it is important that you practice these methods and strategies so that when the transition to adulthood comes, you will be more prepared.

I think we can all agree that consumerism is a long-lasting trend nowadays, and people just want to buy and buy without even thinking if they actually need what they are purchasing. This is also a fast way to increase debt, especially if you don't have a budget. Just to give some actual research, the average person spends about $161 on clothes monthly, and the average child in the U.S. has about $6,000 worth of toys by the time they reach their teenage years (Bowling, 2019). That's a lot of wasted money, in my humble opinion, and this also reveals the lack of budgeting skills most people have. Many of these come from impulse purchases and bad spending habits. But let's look at some ways you can shop smarter.

Let's first look at online shopping, which is something that has been growing over the last few decades with the advent of technology and some companies such as Amazon. However, online shopping made it far easier to compare prices with other online retailers. And this is exactly the first thing you should do. You can quickly go to other websites, search for the same or similar items, and check their prices. This is a great way to get a bargain on certain items. Reading the reviews is also important, which is also something that online shopping makes easier. When reading the reviews of a certain item, if they are simply bad, you tend to give up on the product and move on. If you don't usually read reviews and you like what you see, chances are that you are going to purchase it and possibly be disappointed. Reading reviews stops many people from making purchasing mistakes. Sometimes the reviews don't need to be all that bad, but they might point out the capabilities of that item, which you might find to be of no use to you.

The world of coupons is gigantic, and more people should use it. Coupons allow us to get cheaper prices on certain things. But you have to be careful and only use coupons on things that you were looking for before because many people tend to buy things with coupons that they wouldn't even think about buying if they hadn't seen the coupon. For that, make sure you know what you want, and don't let yourself be persuaded by these marketing tricks. Waiting for a sale, especially an internet sale, might be quite convenient since you can simply sign in and order the items once the sales start, which is far easier than offline shopping. If this is something that you can purchase later, then by all means, you should wait for a sale if you know one is coming.

Always double-check the return policy when you shop online because, especially with clothes, we often purchase the wrong size. However, if you don't know how the return policy works, you might find yourself unable to replace the item. Some return policies last only two weeks, while others might last a month, two, or even three. Either way, you need to make sure you check it and know when you have to send it back. Imagine that you buy a jacket, and the policy states that you have 15 days to return it. The jacket takes eight or nine days to arrive, so chances are that you're not going to be able to return it in time.

Let's move on to purchasing clothes since this is where many people spend a lot of money. The first thing you should do is refer back to your budget and understand how much you can spend on clothes. Without this, chances are that you are going to overspend. Knowing exactly what you need is also important because it stops you from purchasing things that you might like but don't need. If you go to the mall with no clear idea of what you need to buy, you are probably coming back home with too many things and sometimes without the things you need. When shopping for clothes, you need to take your time, especially if you are in a shopping center or mall, and go around other shops to check on prices. If you're looking for a shirt, don't buy the first one you like because it might happen that later on you will find another one that you like more at a cheaper price. So, shop around and come back to the one that you liked more.

Buying clothes off-season tends to be a little cheaper. This can be better done after the season ends because merchants tend to lower their prices so they can sell the remnants of the previous collection and have more space to place the new collection. Alternatively, you can go to thrift stores. I do understand that not everybody likes to purchase clothes at the thrift store, but if you don't mind, it's a great place to find good brands at lower prices. Lastly, you should always go for quality over quantity. It's better to buy one pair of high-quality jeans than four pairs of lower-quality jeans because chances are that those cheap jeans will all wear out faster than the single high-quality one, and you will be back to shopping faster.

Groceries are a necessity but are not a fixed expense, so you could apply strategies and methods that will reduce their cost. The first thing that I would recommend is to always have a grocery list with you when grocery shopping. Planning ahead is fundamental so you don't get caught up in purchasing things that you weren't meant to purchase. It's also important so you don't forget to purchase important goods. It's important that you buy fruits and vegetables locally, not because they are necessarily cheaper (although they might be), but because they are certainly fresher than those you can find in a supermarket. Before you head out to go grocery shopping, have a look at your fridge and cupboards so you don't buy goods that you wouldn't need, and that would eventually be thrown away. Here, you should always plan to avoid wasting food. To do that, everything you buy should have a planned purpose. For instance, don't buy tomatoes if you're not planning on using them next week since chances are they will expire, and you will have to throw them away.

It's always better to buy groceries for the whole household since it's cheaper to buy in bulk instead of going grocery shopping every few days. Bigger packs are usually cheaper than smaller ones. However, you should always check expiration dates as well as prices so things don't go to waste or you buy alternative products that will cost you more.

Once in a while, we need to make big purchases, and these require more thorough planning. I'm talking about cars, fridges, tables, TVs, etc., things that you buy once every few years. And exactly because of that, you need to think more about them. Here, you should be researching as many options as you possibly can and even asking for professional advice if possible. When you are divided about what to purchase, you should know everything you can, from the model to the consumption, reviews, etc. It is even worth talking to friends or family members who have made similar purchases before to help you make a decision and talk to you about the item. But I'll leave the different strategies about big purchases for a dedicated chapter later in the book.

I've mentioned this before briefly, but when making big purchases, you should go for functionalities over big-name brands. The first thing that comes to mind is mobile phones. There might not be any point in purchasing the latest version of an iPhone if you can find another phone that has the same or even more functionalities but whose brand is not as recognizable. Here, it's also important that you look at reviews before purchasing, of course. Usually, with big brands, you rarely pay for how good the item is and pay more for its name. If you can, you should consider purchasing in installments; this is especially true if there's no interest on the items you are purchasing. If the interest is minimal, you can still consider it since you might not be able to purchase the whole amount in one sitting or if this would disrupt your budget and take from your savings.

While you might not really think about having kids, it's important to understand that they will be a sizable part of your budget. This also has to be thought out thoroughly. When shopping for kids, one thing that you should often keep in mind is that, in most cases, you probably don't need to buy anything. I'm mostly talking about toys and other things to spoil your kid. They will probably throw a tantrum, but that's fine; they are kids, after all, and they will get over it. You have to be reasonable and explain to them that they can't have everything they want. However, it's also important that you consider their opinion on certain things. If you want to buy something for them, you should probably take them with you, as it is more likely that they will use it or play with it for longer periods, and you won't need to purchase something else in a short period of time.

How Can You Compare Prices?

As I've noted above, purchasing online or in-store items is a little different, and as such, you should use slightly different ways of comparing prices. Let's start with comparing prices online.

The easiest way to compare prices online is to use a comparison tool. These are usually websites where you can compare online products side by side. There are many different ones that you can use, and amidst so many to choose from, you have to actually use some of them to see which ones you prefer. I tend to use more than one so I can have more information and make a better choice. Some of the most popular ones are Google Shopping, Shopzilla, and Shopping.com. Bear in mind that these are popular ones in the US, there might be different ones in different countries.

A quick Google search will allow you to check out many different comparison websites. Some are better at comparing prices in specific stores, while others are really good at checking certain types of items, so do your research and decide which ones you want to use. Alternatively, you can also use mobile apps if you find them more convenient. Then, once you've decided on what websites or app comparison tools to use, you can go on and type the product in the search bar. Here, you will find that different tools display items and prices differently. You can also look for the type of item or for specific brand products. Usually, the tool will give you some other options to look at. If you don't have any specific brand in mind, you can also search for different categories or departments and browse through the different items.

Then, all you have to do is browse through the different results that appear. Some of these tools allow you to see the number of stores selling a certain product, but you can filter it to look for other results or list them in different orders. Then, you can click on the item that interests you, and a list of different merchants selling the same item will appear. Here, you can filter for the best or lowest price. Keep in mind that the lowest price might not be the best deal you will find. Sometimes the merchant might be more reliable, and you will know you won't have any issues with the product or the delivery. If there's not much of a discrepancy, or if there's a discrepancy between a reputable seller and one that doesn't have a good reputation, I always go for the one with the best reputation. Researching the seller is something that you should always aim to do, especially if you don't know them, regardless of how reputable they are. Usually, you can purchase right from the price comparison page; other times, you might have to go to the merchant's website.

Of course, some people still prefer to compare prices manually, even though they use computers. Here's what you can do: First, you need to make a list of stores that you know are reliable. Before this, you should have a product in mind, and depending on the product you want to purchase, the type of stores you will be listing will be different. Then, you should visit each store's website. Even if you don't know the website, this can easily be found by Googling the name of the store. Every merchant's website has a search bar where you can simply type the name or the kind of product you want, and it will appear. You then proceed to write down the price and the brand. It's always wise to check shipping policies since a product might be cheaper at one merchant than at another, but the shipping price might be a lot higher, which makes the whole item more expensive. Ideally, if you can find a merchant that ships the product for free or you pick it up in-store, that would definitely be the cheapest option. Then, as you do your research and write everything down, you can compare it at the end and check out the best options for you.

Now, when it comes to comparing and calculating prices at the store, it might take a little longer than when done online. This is especially true when you're looking at bigger packages and trying to figure out if the overall price is really that much better than smaller packages. Usually, checking the unit price of the item can give you a better idea of how much you are actually saving. When we talk about unit price, we are usually referring to its cost per quantity. However, here this can mean that the quantity is per item or per unit of measurement, but don't worry, I'll go through all the processes.

In order to calculate the unit price, all you have to do is divide the cost of the product by its quantity (what you are actually receiving by purchasing the package). There are two ways of doing this. The first is, as I've said, calculating the unit price. The first thing to do here is to check the item's total price, which is usually a smaller percentage of the total cost of the packaged product. This can usually be found on the product's label at the store. You might have a coupon, and if you want to calculate the unit price with the coupon, you need to subtract the coupon's value from the overall price before you calculate the unit price. Then, you have to find the quantity that the package has. You can find this on the label of the product. While some goods are sold by item, such as pencils or toilet paper, others will have a unit of measurement, such as liters, ounces, or gallons.

When comparing, it's important to make sure that the two products you are comparing are in the same units of measurement when not compared by item. It is very common that two products you are comparing might be in different units of measurement, which makes it harder to compare. If this is the case, then you will have to convert the units of measurement so they are the same. You can simply use a measurement unit online to figure this out. Let's look at milk, which is sometimes measured in gallons and sometimes in quarts. If a quart of milk is priced at $2 and a gallon is $8, then these two products cost the same because a gallon is four quarts of milk, so $2 x 4 = $8.

You can then divide the total price by the quantity of the item to figure out the unit price. Here, I would say using a calculator would be faster. For instance, if you are looking at a 4-roll pack of toilet paper at $5 and you want to know the unit price, you'd have to divide $5 by 4, so the unit price is $1.25 per roll of toilet paper. Again, most stores have the unit cost on their label, so you don't have to make any calculations, but it is always better to know how it works in case some products don't display that.

The second method is comparing unit prices. Here, to calculate the unit price of the goods you want to purchase, you need to divide the total cost of each good by the quantity in the package they are sold in. So, for example, one package of 4-roll toilet paper is priced at $5, and another package has 6 rolls and is priced at $6.30. Which one do you think has the cheaper unit price? First, you need to calculate $5/4, which is $1.25 a roll. Then you need to divide $6.30 by 6, which is $1.05. The 6-roll package of toilet paper is cheaper. In general, the product with the lowest unit price is the best value, but you also have to look at the quality. If the quality is similar, then you should go for the cheaper one, but if not, you need to try and understand if it's worth it to pay less for worse quality. While these two methods have the same results, the first allows you to calculate unit prices to understand the price of each unit, and the second allows you to take two items with the same function but different prices and figure out which one has the best value.

How to Save Money on Bills and Other Purchases?

The best way to increase your savings is to make a budget, but there are other ways you can retain more of the money you earn and add it to your savings, such as by cutting your energy bills. You might have heard your parents talking around the house about the incredibly high cost of bills at the moment. While this might change by the time you have to pay your own bills, you can always try to save as much as you can. One thing that you might not be aware of is that usually, energy bills such as electricity and gas are paid through direct debit from your card, and this can be changed. What energy companies usually take is an estimate to cover what you have spent. This is because we use more energy in certain months than we do in others; for instance, in the winter, we tend to use more energy so we can warm our houses. However, while some months you might have a debt on your energy account, other times you might have credit. But you need to keep checking that to make sure you are not overpaying your energy bill or falling into a large debt. Sometimes, the energy company increases the direct debit on your card, and this might be for some reason, such as if you've moved on to a more expensive bill or if your contract with them has expired. They usually put you on a higher tariff. You need to contact them to renew your contract or look for a new energy provider. It can also happen that you are in a variable tariff contract, in which case the rates have increased. If you don't want that to happen, you would have to get into a fixed tariff, which might look more expensive but is often better since you know exactly how much you will be paying per unit of energy. If your energy use has increased, this could also be another reason why your direct debit has gone up too. If you're not sure why the direct debit has increased, you should always contact your energy provider to make sure there's no mistake on their behalf.

Now that this is out of the way let's get into the real tips. Heating your home is where most people spend the most energy. So, you might ask, What is the most energy-efficient way to heat a room? Well, central heating is definitely the most efficient way to do this, but not all properties have it. This is especially true if you're renting and you don't have another choice but to use what is provided to you. However, if central heating is not an option and you only need to heat the room you are in, then a portable heater is definitely the second-best choice. However, you need to pick one that is cost-efficient. You can use the price comparison tips I've mentioned above to pick the best one. Ideally, you'd pick a portable heater that has a timer and a good thermostat so it doesn't overheat and you don't spend too much energy and money on it.

Cooking is another thing where a lot of energy is consumed. Here, electric ovens are far more efficient than gas ones. The same is true for electric hobs. However, here, more efficiency doesn't mean cheaper since gas tends to be cheaper than electricity. However, air fryers and microwaves (for small things) tend to save you more money in the long run. Apart from that, there's not much you can do when it comes to cooking besides trying not to have your oven on for too long and preparing everything before so you can cook as fast as you can. However, if and when you have your own property, purchasing energy-efficient appliances can really make a difference in your energy bill. Again, when doing this, make sure you compare all the appliances so you can have the most energy-efficient and not the cheapest appliance since, in the long run, you'd be paying more.

Insulating your home is also a good way to save energy. Once again, if you're renting, there's not a lot you can do. But when you're looking for properties to rent, you should keep in mind that properties that are better insulated tend to waste less energy. So, properties that have the attic insulated, have draft proofing installed, and have double-glazing tend to be more energy efficient.

Not everything is gas and electricity when it comes to bills, and there are other things such as cellphone contracts, broadband, and insurance where you can also reduce costs. When it comes to an internet connection, unless you are out of contract, in my experience, there's no point in changing because you most certainly have to pay an early opt-out fee. However, if your contract runs out, this is an excellent opportunity to get a cheaper and faster internet connection. If you don't have fiber

Money Skills for Teens

yet, then this is the best time to upgrade. While it usually costs the same as standard broadband, it is a lot faster and more reliable. When it comes to your cell phone, you should keep an eye on your data and check if you are really using all the data you are purchasing every month or if you can reduce that data and the price you're paying for it. While many providers offer high amounts of data and sometimes even unlimited data, most people use between 5 and 10 GB, so there's no need to purchase all that data most of the time.

One thing that I had to learn with time and experience is that when it comes to cell phones and broadband, you can haggle the price. Yes, nothing is really set in stone, and if you've been a customer with them for quite some time, your chances are even higher to get a better price. If you think that negotiating can be overwhelming, you can do it over a text chat or email. But to be prepared, you should compare the services with those of other providers so you can back up your negotiations.

At some point in your adult life, you will have home and car insurance. These are needs because you need your valuables protected. The best way to reduce them is when it's time to renew them. Obviously, when you got them the first time, you should have gone through comparison websites and checked out the best available deal for you. But this insurance industry is always on the move, and when it is time to renew, chances are that you will find a better deal. You do the same thing you've done before and do your research with the help of comparison websites. Even if you're not near renewal, you can always check with other insurance companies, and perhaps an early switch might be able to save you some money. Here, you have to take into account the cost of early cancellation, of course, but if the rival's prices are that much better, you should consider switching. The way you pay is also important. These usually come in monthly or annual payments, and annual payments are almost always cheaper. But this is a calculation that you can do quickly; simply divide the total amount of the annual insurance payment by 12 and check if it's cheaper than paying monthly. It's also important to have a close look at the extras insurance companies often add to the contract; most of the time, you won't need those extra covers, and you can save money that way. A good piece of advice that I would give and that you could probably follow is to put the name of someone with more driving experience if you don't have that much experience because young and inexperienced drivers tend to pay more.

Fuel is a necessity if you, like many people, rely on your own method of transportation. The question that should be on your mind when the time comes is, How can I drive and spend less on fuel? Well, the first thing that comes to mind here is to drive as smoothly as possible, try to preserve momentum, and don't accelerate if there's no need to. This might not be much of a tip, but trust me, in the long run, it will save you a lot of fuel. For instance, if you have a good idea of what's ahead of you when you drive, you will better control your acceleration or know when you should and when you shouldn't. Essentially, anticipating what is ahead and not using braking and acceleration for no reason. By the way, breaking also wastes fuel since you then have to use more fuel to accelerate. While in the U.S., manual gears are not very common, if you do ever drive one, shifting gears as soon as possible will ease the work the engine will have to do and, with that, consume less fuel too. In fact, if you drive a new-ish car, they already indicate when it is best to shift gears. Plus, new cars have other modes where you can switch to Eco, for instance, which will allow you to consume less fuel too.

Perhaps you've seen your parents use the car on cold days, and they run the engine while staying stationary so the engine heats up. This is hardly needed with new cars because the engine is designed to heat up way faster. Only use air conditioning when strictly necessary since these waste quite some energy, but using it once in a while will also prevent it from having issues more often. Heated seats are hardly ever necessary unless you live in a very cold place. These seats also consume a lot of energy, most of the time unnecessarily. Also, checking your tire pressure can often help you save some fuel since the more deflated the tires are, the more energy the engine wastes.

Reducing your overall spending as well as your bills can have a huge impact on your savings. It all starts with making informed decisions when purchasing goods or services. Understanding how to shop smartly and how to compare prices is fundamental to all of this. There are many comparison websites where you can find the most varied goods to do your research. You also have to have a clear idea of your needs and wants, and when shopping, it is best to bring a list with you so you don't forget anything and don't spend unnecessarily. With the tips I talked about on how to save money, while I don't expect you to memorize everything or even apply all of them, it is important that you are aware of them and that when the time comes, you know the things you can do to increase your savings.

CHAPTER 6

CREDIT, CREDIT CARDS, AND DEBT MANAGEMENT

> *Don't let your mouth write no check that your tail can't cash.*
>
> — *Bo Diddley*

C redit, credit cards, and debt might be something that scares you. Perhaps you don't fully understand it, but you've probably heard your parents talking about it, someone in your family, or even on TV. The truth is, while debt and credit cards can have a negative effect on your finances, they also have a positive side. I've briefly talked about it before, but now I'm delving more into the topic.

What Is Credit, and Why Is it Important?

While the word "credit" might have different meanings in the financial sector, it often means an agreement where an individual, also called a borrower, gets money but at the same time states that they will give it back at a later date, usually with interest. But credit can also refer to the credit score or credit history of someone, so you can have good or bad credit. Don't worry; I will get to that.

There are many different forms of credit, but the most common one is a credit card; however, there are also mortgages, car loans, and personal loans. With a credit card, you have a line of credit where you have a certain amount that you can spend on that specific card. There are two main types of credit, and all of the forms of credit I've mentioned above fall within one of them. These are revolving or installment loans. Revolving credit is, for instance, a credit card where you can continuously borrow more and more money as long as you pay the minimum balance at a certain date. An installment credit is, for example, a mortgage where you have fixed amounts to pay every month, and you don't continuously take out money. Usually, this comes as a lump sum. Both of these usually have interest.

When somebody says that credit is important, it usually refers to your credit score or history. This is what banks and other financial institutions refer to when deciding if they should lend you money or not. They often look at your credit report, which often states things like payment history, which tells them how often you make credit payments on time; credit utilization, which means how much of your credit in your credit cards you have used (usually the less, the better); length of credit history, which refers to the amount of time you have had credit, whether it is a credit card or a car loan (where usually the longer, the better); credit mix, which is how diversified your credit is, such as credit cards, mortgages, car loans, etc.; and new credit, which tells them how often you take on a new credit card (opening too many credit accounts throughout a small period of time is usually not good).

The health of your credit is important because it opens the doors for many things, such as applying for a credit card, purchasing a house, renting a house or apartment, applying for a job, buying a car, or even starting a business. This is because, for most of these, you need to borrow money, and the lender is going to look at your credit score and credit history to understand if it is safe for them to actually lend you the money. It's also important to note that even with a bad credit score, financial institutions can still lend you money, but oftentimes this will have a higher interest rate. This is something that you want to avoid because it means you'd be spying on a lot more than what you are borrowing.

So, as you can see, having a credit card is not so bad and allows you to build your credit score and credit history. However, you have to manage it properly.

How Can You Manage Your Credit Properly and Responsibly?

Managing your credit responsibly is the important part. You want to get a high credit score so you can borrow higher amounts and pay less interest. If you miss payment dates, default, or file for bankruptcy, your credit score will decrease. This is also true if you, as I said, use too much of your credit or open too many credit card accounts in a short period of time.

So, in order to manage your credit responsibly, I have a few tips for you. Always make your credit card payments and other credit payments on time. While paying more than the minimum payment is better because it means in the long run, you will be paying less, you have to at least pay the minimum amount. In fact, if you don't make a single payment on time, this can stay on your credit report for years to come. Another thing you should not do is spend more than you can afford to repay. It seems easy enough, but many people fall for this mistake. You should never live off your credit card unless you have absolutely no money for your basic necessities. What I like to do to ensure I never miss a payment is to set up a reminder or a direct debit.

Credit cards should strictly be used to build credit, so you should pay small amounts with them and not big amounts unless you have the money ready to pay them. One last thing: you should keep your old credit card accounts open even if you don't use them because they count toward your length of credit history.

How Can You Build a Good Credit Score?

Some of the things you can do to build or maintain a great credit score have already been mentioned. But there are other things. For instance, getting on your electoral roll is an easy way to get some points on your credit score. This is often used by lenders to check your address as well as your name and to verify if everything is up-to-date.

Getting credit, as I've mentioned, is also a great way to improve your score. But remember to take out a small and manageable amount so you can pay it back on time and fully, and don't get overwhelmed by the amount of debt. Sometimes, you can get a score boost too. The three major credit bureau companies are Experian, Equifax, and TransUnion, and sometimes all you need to do is link your current account to one of the credit bureau companies. This is an easier way for those companies to know how well you manage your credit. When it comes to credit score levels, what you want to achieve is "excellent," but a "very good" or even a "good" level of credit score points can give you quite some rewards. Here's a table of the credit score range for your credit level:

Poor	300–579
Fair	580–669
Good	670–739
Very good	740–799
Excellent	800–850

Here's a summarized list of things you can do to increase your credit score, besides some of the things I've already mentioned before:

- Setting up automatic bill payments
- Paying down credit balances
- Getting a credit-builder loan
- Disputing credit report inaccuracies
- Keeping old credit card accounts open
- Limiting the number of lines of credit you get
- Paying off credit card balances every single month
- Keeping track of your credit score
- Adding to your credit mix
- Adding rent payments to your credit score report
- Asking for an increase on your credit card limit

How Can You Manage Your Credit Card Debt?

Although most people understand the risks of taking on large amounts of debt, there are times when they fall into these debts and struggle to pay them. It's important that you don't shy away from or try to ignore this problem. In fact, you have to face it and look for solutions. While it might look bad, and it is, it's not the end of the world, and there are things you can do. But first, let me explain to you the process if you fall into overwhelming amounts of debt and can't pay them.

Every credit card is covered by the Consumer Credit Protection Act, which means that lending companies such as banks and other financial institutions have to follow some rules if the debtor (you) is struggling to pay. So, it all starts by not paying the minimum amount in a month, after which your bank will contact you and demand that you pay that month's amount. If you don't, then they will put your account in default. If you still don't pay, then they might bring in a debt collection agent to recover the money you owe. It sounds a little scary, but at this point, you've had enough time to do something about it, as I'll explain below.

Banks and other financial institutions, to help their customers that are struggling, can do a few things: they can give you a credit card payment "holiday," which means you are "off the hook" for three months (obviously, you still have to pay it). They often make sure that your credit score is not affected during this three-month period. And they can also increase your credit card limit; however, you should be careful about this because it means that later on, you can incur more debt.

Now, onto things that you can do to pay off your credit card. The first thing you have to do is really try to understand your finances. This means fully understanding what you can afford every month. You have to budget! If you have been forgetting to budget, you will have to do it because this is the only way you can understand how much you can spend. When doing your budget, make sure you set aside a part of your income so you can pay your debt. You have to absolutely stop using your credit card. You can't afford to incur more debt than you already have.

You can also negotiate your credit card debt by contacting your bank and explaining everything to them. Here, you can also tell them how much you can pay each month, and believe it or not, many banks agree to some of the terms you might bring up and even agree to an affordable repayment plan.

How Can You Deal With Debt Collectors?

Hopefully, this will never happen to you, and if you ever have an overwhelming amount of debt, you will follow the steps I've written above to avoid it. But if you are ever in a situation where you have to deal with debt collectors, there are also a few things that you can do. Usually, debt collectors will contact you about an unpaid debt. Remember, you have to face your problems here, and hiding is never the solution because it can get much worse. While you have to deal with them, it's important that you understand your rights under the Fair Debt Collection Practices Act (FDCPA). For instance, debt collectors cannot threaten you, lie to you, or insult you in any way (they can't even say they will sue you if they don't intend to do so). They can't add interest to your debt unless it is written in the contract on your credit card or other agreement, and they can't threaten to take your property (or even take it) unless the property is served as collateral when you take out a loan.

They have to first notify you in writing (this could be by mail or online) at least within five days of any contact you've had with them. And they have to give you 30 days from their notification to ask for any more information about the debt. Also, there have been some recent rule changes where debt collectors can't call you more than seven times in a single week, and they can't talk to you from any social media platform.

You can also check if your debt is actually valid. This means that you need to check the notification the debt collector gave you and make sure that it is yours. It could be that the amount is wrong, or perhaps you've already paid the debt. Understanding your statute of limitations is also important. This means that debt collectors have a certain amount of time to claim the debt, but this amount of time differs depending on the state you are in. If they come after you after that statute of limitations has expired, you don't have to pay, and in fact, you can sue them.

Of course, you can always consider negotiating with a debt collector. This is after you've checked your statute of limitations and know for sure the debt is yours, but you can't afford to pay everything right away, you can try and negotiate with them. For instance, you can try to get an agreement where you pay back the debt in installments, or you can propose a settlement where they will have to agree not to pay the full amount of debt. However, if the debt is legitimate, you should always try to pay it in full, even if it is in installments, because this will hurt your credit score.

If you believe that a debt collector is harassing you, you can send a cease and desist letter, which basically tells them to stop contacting you. This can be done if the statute of limitations has run out or you don't have any assets, which means you won't be able to pay anything even if they sue you and you lose.

Credit is quite important to understand and to build as soon as we possibly can. Having good credit allows us to borrow money for large expenses such as buying a car or a house. However, credit can also be quite dangerous if we don't pay attention to it. We could become overwhelmed with the amount of debt we accumulate, which would make our financial lives quite complicated. It's important that we always pay back whatever we have borrowed and don't borrow more than we can pay; that's how debts get out of hand. But again, we need to use our credit cards to build a good credit history. If, for some reason, you accumulate more debt than you can pay, you should never try to hide from it, as it will always find you. This is one of those problems that don't go away until we face them. As I've explained in this chapter, there are ways that you can actively work to reduce your debt, such as by fully understanding your finances, creating a budget, or, in extreme cases, contacting your bank.

CHAPTER 7

INVESTING

> Invest for the long haul. Don't get too greedy,
> and don't get too scared.
>
> — Shelby M.C. Davies

nvesting is another one of those things that people get a little scared of when mentioned. Many believe it's a way to lose all your money. But I assure you that those people have never invested in their lives. Yes, it is true that you can lose money if you don't have the faintest idea of what you're doing, but you can also make a lot of money just by understanding the basics.

The Basics You Need to Know

People have been investing for many years, and it is a tried and true way to put your money to work for you. You should be able to invest at regular intervals as you get your income, and once you know the basics and have the possibilities, it should be a part of your budget to set aside some money to invest. This is also the reason why investing as soon as you possibly can might allow you to make a lot of money. The thing is, you don't need a large amount of money to start; you can simply begin with $10, $25, or even a single dollar. But of course, you need to know what you're doing, and while many people feel daunted about the stock market and investing in general, the basics are not that hard to grasp.

Now, before we get into it, I want to talk about the three most common ways of investing: stocks, mutual funds, and bonds. You've probably heard about these but don't know exactly what they mean.

Let's start with what I believe to be the most popular of them all: stocks. These are often referred to as equity, and essentially, they are a small part of a business or corporation. Every time you purchase a fraction of such an organization in the stock market (where they are sold), you are buying what is called a share. This officially tells you that you are the owner of a portion of a corporation. In case your head is still wrapped up in what you might have heard about stocks, the trading of these is regulated by the government to protect investors like you from fraud. Now, businesses and corporations issue these shares or stocks to raise funds for their businesses so they can operate. Now, to buy stocks, you have to get them through stock exchanges, or more commonly, the stock market, such as the New York Stock Exchange (NYSE) or the Nasdaq. However, you don't have to physically go there, and nowadays, buying and selling stocks is easier than ever. There are many mobile applications that you can download, sign up for, and use from your mobile phone. For instance, a popular one is called Robinhood. You have to be over 18 years old to hold an account and trade stocks, plus you have to give ID proof and proof of address, as well as have a bank account. Although you might be asking, How do I earn income from owning stocks? There are two ways you can do this. The first, and probably simpler, is when the stock increases in value. Say you buy a single share of Microsoft for $100, and after a year, the value has risen to $150. If you sold at that time, you would take $150 or a $50 profit. Another way is through dividends, but this is only specific to some stocks. In fact, Microsoft also offers dividends on its stocks. Dividends are a small percentage of the value of the stock paid to shareholders or investors. This is usually paid every quarter, and you can check how much the corporation pays to the investors by looking at the dividend yield (also, most of this information can be looked up online or through your brokerage app). For instance, using the same example above, if you have a share of Microsoft valued at $100 and the dividend yield is 1%, you'd get paid $1.

Getting Started

Before you get started trading stocks, you need to learn the basics, of course, but there are other things that you need to establish. The first thing you should do is define your tolerance for risk. In basic terms, tolerance for risk is what you can afford to lose when investing. There are many categories within stocks that can tell you more or less about their risk (obviously, investments are never 100% sure); for example, you have large, medium, and small capitalization stocks, meaning the larger the capitalization, the smaller the volatility of the price, but also the fewer chances you have to make big money. Then you have value stocks and aggressive stocks, and all of these have different levels of risk. Once you know your risk tolerance, you can start really looking at the types of stocks to buy.

You also have to understand what your investment goals are. For most people, investments mean the long term. This means that you usually purchase some stock that you believe will go up over a long period of time (say five years, for instance. Other, more professional investors, like to invest in the short- or medium-term. This is something that I wouldn't recommend, especially if you're just starting out. Of course, your goals could also change over time; for instance, you might start by simply trying to increase the amount of money you have, while later on, you could try to get an income from your investments through dividends. Other more concrete investments could be purchasing a car or a house, saving for retirement, or paying for tuition.

Then, you have to determine your investment style, which basically means how you want to manage your portfolio (all your stocks). Many people prefer to purchase something and forget about it, meaning that they are not constantly checking it. You believe that they will continue to slowly go up. Others prefer to be more thorough, check their portfolios more often, and tweak here and there for maximum profitability. There's also something called the robo-advisor, which is an automated tool where you insert your goals, and add money to them (often through a stockbroker's app), and the robo-advisor tweaks your investments to align with your goals. Lastly, you can also pay for a financial advisor to give you some tips. However, these can be quite expensive, and unless you have a lot of money invested, they are probably not worth it.

Then, you will have to choose your investment account. Here, you have retirement plans usually sponsored by your employer, such as a 401(k), where you can choose from stocks, bonds, mutual funds, etc. However, I'll talk about all of this later. You can also choose to open a taxable account or IRA with a brokerage instead of an employer-sponsored one. These can also be retirement accounts, and you can have your own as well as employer-sponsored ones. Robo-advisors also have a specific account.

Lastly, you have to really learn the basics and learn how to diversify so you can reduce the risk. Diversification is perhaps the most important thing when it comes to investment. Let me give you an example of diversification. Say, you have $1000 invested in the stock market, but all the money is on Microsoft stocks. Here, your portfolio has zero diversification because everything is in one single stock. What happens if Microsoft has a bad quarter or some negative news? All your portfolios will suffer. But now, you have put only $250 on Microsoft, $250 on Nvidia, $250 on Apple, and $250 on Facebook. There's some more diversification, without a doubt, because even if Microsoft goes down momentarily, you have the other three stocks to keep your portfolio from free-falling. However, as you might have noticed, all of these stocks are in the technology sector. What if this specific sector is having a rough time for whatever reason? What if you put $250 on Microsoft, $250 on Apple, $250 on Coca-Cola, and $250 on Fiat? Your diversification would be a lot better, and you'd reduce the risk of losing a lot of your investment money.

Mutual funds are managed funds that use money from several investors to invest in stocks. This way, you don't have to manage it yourself. It's also important to understand that in these mutual funds, there can be stocks as well as bonds (which I will mention later in the chapter). These funds are managed by professional money managers, and their goal is to try and maximize gains for the investors, although every mutual fund has a different way of investing, such as being risky or risk averse, and the securities (both stocks and bonds) can be tailored depending on the mutual stock. For instance, you might choose a mutual fund whose premise is to invest in green stocks and bonds. This means that the companies the manager invests in are environmentally friendly. This also means that when you gain or lose money, so do all the other investors in the mutual fund.

However, you must be thinking, How are mutual funds priced? After all, they must have a price since you have to invest a certain amount of money, right? Well, you can look at it as if every time you invest in a mutual fund, a share of it is the average of the prices of all stocks and bonds within the fund. So, for example, if you invest in a mutual fund with two stocks (which is impossible since they usually have more, but bear with me for the sake of explanation) and one stock is currently priced at $200 and the other at $100, a share of the mutual fund would be $150. So, in other words, when you invest in a mutual fund, you are investing in many different stocks and bonds, which is good for diversity. You can also get income from dividends when investing in a mutual fund that holds stocks that distribute dividends.

As I've said, there are many different types of mutual funds, but I'll give some examples of the most common ones. Stock funds, as the name indicates, invest almost exclusively in stocks. Of course, here you will have many more subcategories, at least as many as there are subcategories of stocks and companies. For instance, you might have growth funds that invest in companies that focus on growth, but they usually don't pay dividends. However, you are more likely to gain from the increase in stock price.

Index funds also exclusively invest in stocks but focus on index stocks. These are like mutual funds that you can purchase straight away from the stock market, which can also be called ETFs. One of the largest ones is the S&P 500, which tracks the value of the 500 largest companies in the U.S. ETFs are also an excellent option if you want to diversify your portfolio, and there are many different types.

Balanced funds are a hybrid type of mutual fund that has stocks, bonds, and sometimes even other investment vehicles.

Bonds can be seen as fixed-income investments. They are loans made by a part of a government (for instance, a local government) or a corporation to raise funds. In this particular case, you are the one loaning the money to these entities, and in return (after some time), they will give you back the money plus interest. As you might have guessed, bonds have an end date, which is the date the loan (called the principal) has to be paid back to you. These are called fixed-income because you know for sure they will be paid back, and you know when. Bonds are also much more risk-averse than stocks in mutual funds; however, they are not risk-free, especially bonds from corporations, because they can default. However, this is rare, and even more rare, if you purchase a government bond since these almost never default. Government bonds are issued at literally all levels, so you can have, as I said, local governments, but you also have federal government bonds. Because these are a lot safer, the profit is usually a lot less than in stocks, for instance. Governments usually issue bonds to pay for infrastructure such as schools, hospitals, roads, etc. While corporations might do it to expand their business or raise capital for a new product launch. When you purchase a loan, you have all the necessary information, such as the expiration date, principal per bond, and interest rate (called the coupon rate), so you can clearly understand what the benefits are and how much you can actually receive back. However, after you've purchased a bond, you can resell it at a higher price, or you can also buy bonds from other investors and not directly from the source.

There are other types of bonds. I've already mentioned corporate bonds that are issued by companies. Governmental bonds are solely issued by the U.S. Treasury, and municipal bonds are issued by municipalities and states. Then, you can also have agency bonds, which are issued by government-affiliated organizations.

What Is Compound Interest When Investing?

Compound interest is a very interesting concept that you should be fully aware of because it can allow you to increase your money and wealth. Compound interest can be seen often in savings accounts but also when investing. Many savings accounts only earn interest on the initial deposit. For instance, if you deposit $100 and the interest rate is 5%, after a month, you will have $105. The next month, you will have $110 because the interest is only applied to the initial deposit of $100. However, if that savings account had compound interest, the second month's interest would be applied to the $105, so, you'd have $110.25, and in the third month, you'd have $115.76 instead of $115. While this might not look much, it actually is because if you leave the money for a long time, you're incrementally increasing your money. This, added to the large amount, makes a massive difference in your earnings. Compound interest is often referred to as having interest in the interest. In other words, with compound interest, your money grows faster than if you had applied simple interest.

In investments, you can choose to have a broker's account with a dividend reinvestment plan, also known as DRIP. This automatically reinvests any dividend you receive. This is why, even though you might prefer growth stocks, dividends can really boost your returns.

The "magic" about compound interest is that because it accumulates interest from the previous month (or periods), it grows exponentially, meaning that the accelerating rate is always increasing. These periods, we call compound interest periods, are the intervals of time between when interest is added to the investment or your account. Now, this can come in different ways: annually, semi-annually, quarterly, monthly, or daily. Even if the account you have accrued compound interest daily, often you get paid monthly, and while it's daily, the additional interest is added to when the previous interest gets to the account. So, as you might imagine, the more frequent the compounding interest is, the better for you. But, as you probably figured too, if you are a borrower, compound interest works against you, and when it comes to the frequency of compound interest, you want as sparsely as possible. So, when looking at the benefits of compounding interest, it can help us build wealth in the long term, whether it is through investments or savings, and it mitigates inflation. However, if you are the borrower, compounding interest is not beneficial. It's also important to note that the returns you earn are taxable. Let's look at a table illustrating how much you'd get with compound interest. Here, your initial investment is $5000, and it has a 3% monthly interest for one year (12 months).

Month	Interest	Accrued Interest	Balance
0			$5,000
1	$150	$150.00	$5,150.00
2	$154.50	$304.50	$5,304.50
3	$159.14	$463.64	$5,463.64
4	$163.91	$627.54	$5,627.54
5	$168.83	$796.37	$5,796.37
6	$173.89	$970.26	$5,970.26
7	$179.11	$1,149.37	$6,149.37
8	$184.48	$1,333.85	$6,333.85
9	$190.02	$1,523.87	$6,523.87
10	$195.72	$1,719.58	$6,719.58
11	$201.59	$1,921.17	$6,921.17
12	$207.64	$2,128.80	$7,128.80

As you can see, the accrued interest as well as the interest increase exponentially which by the end of the year has grown quite significantly. If you were to have only simple interest at the exact same rate, your interest would always be fixed at $150 a month. By the end of the twelve months with compound interest, you're earning $207.64 by simply not touching your money.

Long-Term Investment Strategies

There are quite a few strategies to invest in; some are short-term, others long-term, but as you're starting out, I'm going to talk about long-term ones because they require less knowledge of the market and are far safer.

The "ride a winner" strategy means that in your portfolio, you'd have a really good winner," meaning that one of your stocks was really increasing, and you'd only consider selling it after it increased tenfold. However, you have to be quite disciplined and do your due diligence because even if a stock is going to increase ten times, there will be periods where it will go down before going back up, and you need to resist the temptation to sell it. In other words, you have to believe in the stock you've bought and not sell it because it went down a little.

Selling a loser is another long-term strategy where you essentially have to come to terms with the fact that a stock is not going to go back up (at least not any time soon) and cut your losses before it does more damage to your portfolio. I'm talking about drastic or continuous losses, not simply losing a few dollars. Also, you need to understand what is going on in the market to understand the reason behind some stocks losing value before deciding to sell.

Again, don't panic if the stock goes down for a little bit; these are short-term movements, and they are part of the market. You have to zoom out and take a look at what is happening in the big picture of the stock. Also, you should never chase a stock that has increased exponentially within a week. For instance, you see a stock that has increased 50% in the last week, and you have the urge to buy it because it's going up so fast. But chances are that you already lost the ride, and once you buy it, it might come crashing down or won't increase that much anymore. Stick to your strategy and do your due diligence on the stocks you've bought.

Dollar-cost averaging is quite a common strategy in the investment world, and it's often used to manage the price risk of your investments. You apply this strategy every time you're purchasing investments such as stocks or ETFs, and instead of purchasing five shares of a certain stock at one time and at a single price point, you purchase them at different times. So, you're buying that same investment at regular intervals and in smaller parts, independent of the price. Let me give you an example: if you buy two Microsoft shares at $100, your average cost per share is $100, but in the next month, the shares drop 50%, and your share value drops from $200 (since you had two shares) to $100. But what if you bought one share of Microsoft for $100, and the next month you bought it for $50? A month went by, and there was no significant price change; this would be because your average cost per share was $75, and so your investment only dropped 25% instead of 50%. Essentially, you are averaging the cost of your investments by diluting the price point and making them more secure. At the end of the day, you still have the same number of shares, but you bought them, on average, at a cheaper price.

Lastly, you have to focus on the future. You have to study the companies and try to understand where they will be in 5 to 10 years. Understand their business model, read the news, and look at their quarterly and annual reports so you have a better chance of making money.

Investing is a very important part of your finances, and fortunately, people are starting to be more involved in it than other generations were. It is not a place where you lose money; it can happen, but if you know what you are doing, it is often a place where you can make quite a lot of money. As I've mentioned, there are many different options when it comes to investing, such as stocks, bonds, and mutual funds, but a mix of them will make your portfolio more diverse and give you a much better chance at creating returns for you. I would advise you to start with mutual funds because they are more risk-resistant, and you don't have to pick your investments yourself; instead, you have a professional do it for you. Then, I would move on to stocks once you understand the market better and how everything works and have more confidence in your skills. Compound interest is a great way to make returns, and you should use it as often as you can, whether it is in your savings accounts or through your investments, because in the long run, it can make you a lot more money than using simple interest.

In the following chapter, I'm going to talk about insurance, what it is, why it is so important, and the different types of insurance you can have.

CHAPTER 8

INSURANCE

> *Because of the risks, the insurance premium may not be.*
>
> — *Dwayne Brown*

nsurance is an important aspect of life as well as finances if you're looking to protect your assets, your property, or even your family from financial risks. We tend to have a greater peace of mind when we have insurance that can protect us and maintain us financially secure from many risks that life might bring us.

For instance, without car insurance, we would have to bear the burden of paying for all the expenses of the car in case we had a car accident. The same with health insurance which can really cripple our finances. It's quite simple to understand how insurance works. You pay a fee, whether it is monthly or annually, it depends, and the insurance covers the majority of the things that can happen. Of course, this depends on the insurance you have and the many add-ons you might want to have.

Understanding Insurance

As I said, insurance is quite easy to understand, but its benefits are far greater than you might think. For instance, insurance plans might help you pay medical bills, emergencies, hospitalizations, and any medical care you might need in the future. If you don't have that, and with the lack of free healthcare in the U.S., you and your family can be really drained of savings. There's also life insurance that gives money to the surviving members of the family. This is especially good if the person who passed away was the sole earner of the household. This way, the family can pay any debts, mortgages, or anything else. It might not be something that you think too much about now, but once you have family and kids, you will definitely try to inform yourself about it.

Life insurance can also help you with retirement planning and stay financially independent throughout your retirement. Property insurance allows you to get paid in case of a natural disaster or any other kind that might destroy your property or if someone gets in and steals valuable things. Your insurance has coverage for that. It is a really good thing to have because life is unpredictable, and you don't know when something might happen. It is always best to be prepared.

What are the Types of Insurance Out There?

There are quite a lot, but I'm just going to name a few. While some of them I've already mentioned, I'll just go a little deeper in explaining what they are.

Life insurance, as I've said, is what can safeguard your family in the event of death. In simple words, it can help the family financially, usually with a lump sum of money that is paid to them if something happens. Health insurance covers medical expenses in many different ways. As I've mentioned, treatments, hospitalization, or any other treatments you'd need afterward. Child plans are great because they work as a sort of savings for when the child is ready to go to college or university.

Home insurance covers any damages to your property caused by accidents, natural calamities, mishaps, and pretty much anything else. And auto insurance is for vehicles, and these are mandatory. These cover accidents with other vehicles as well as natural disasters. They also protect damages to third parties during an accident where you might have hurt somebody while driving your car.

Evaluating Your Options Before Purchasing Insurance

Like many other things when it comes to finances, it's important that you properly evaluate insurance before purchasing it. The first thing to do is assess what you need. Having a look at your requirements is key to fully comprehending the policies you need. Usually, the most important thing is to protect yourself and your family financially. For instance, if you want to save money for your kid's education or buy a property, you should perhaps look into a unit-linked insurance plan or ULIP. An insurance pension account, on the other hand, will give you an income once you retire.

However, purchasing your insurance is not something that you should do and forget. You have to review it throughout your life and change it as your needs change. Essentially, you should try to protect yourself and your family from all financial liabilities. For example, if you are purchasing life insurance, you need to make sure it is big enough to cover any debts.

As with many other things, comparing plans will give you a much better idea of the insurance you are purchasing. There are many different solutions out there, and it is important that you take your time to choose the best one, as well as the one where you pay the lowest premiums. However, I believe that the benefits of a plan are more important than its pricing. I know many of us don't read the terms and conditions, but when it comes to insurance, it's crucial that you do. Not only read them but understand them fully.

Buying insurance is not as hard as it seems, but you need to be absolutely sure of what you are buying and that you are making the best possible decision for you and your family.

In the next chapter, I'll be talking about big purchases, whether material or to improve ourselves and others, such as paying for college. I'm going to go through how you can plan for significant purchases, understand the financing options and explore the different strategies you can use.

CHAPTER 9

BIG PURCHASES AND PAYING FOR COLLEGE

> *Education is the most powerful weapon which you can use to change the world.*
>
> — *Nelson Mandela*

B ig purchases don't always mean buying properties and cars (however, I will start with those); they also mean investing in our future. For that, you need to plan carefully so you don't end up making mistakes that might affect you in the future.

How Can You Plan For Big Purchases?

When planning for big purchases (yes, I'm talking houses or cars), you know that you will need significant funding. For that, you really need to think about how you are going to actually do it. You need to think about how much money you can put up front and all the consequences that entail.

The first thing to do is assess your needs, goals, and timeline. The latter is especially important because you might have to pay it for quite a few years, such as on a property through a mortgage. Determining the true cost of what you have to pay is also important. For example, if you are thinking about purchasing a property, you need to determine the down payment; if you are purchasing a car, you need to figure out the upfront money. So, for that, you also have to think about how long you have to save (a budget with this in mind is your best tool). For instance, you need to save $20,000 in the next two years so you can pay the down payment for a property. How much do you need to be saving every month? You have to save roughly $850. From there, you have to budget and make changes so you can reach your goal.

One thing that I like to do is set up a separate account. This means staying away from your regular savings, your checking account, and your emergency fund. Ideally, you could put it to work earning interest in a savings account. But the goal is to have it separate so you can clearly see it growing and know that you are getting closer to your goal every month.

However, it's important that you don't ignore your other financial goals, so don't make unrealistic goals for large purchases. It's crucial that you build yourself a good and strong financial foundation before taking on large purchases.

Financing Options When Making Big Purchases

If you're buying a property, the best financing option is definitely a mortgage through a bank. Again, you have to shop around and talk to several banks and financial institutions so you can get the best possible mortgage with lower interest rates.

Now, if you're purchasing another big purchase that is not a property, there are options. For instance, if you want to purchase a car, car financing is possibly the best option. There are different options when it comes to this particular financing option. For instance, you have a car loan where you choose the loan amount that you need and for how long you need it. If approved, this money will be paid into your account, and you will purchase the car. Then, you pay this loan in installments. Having a great credit score will ensure you have the best possible interest rates and that you are approved.

You also have a hire purchase, or HP, where you have to also pay in installments (both the loan and the interest), but unlike a car loan, usually, you have to pay something upfront (usually 10% of the car); however, the larger the upfront money, the lower the interest rates are. Here, you can also choose the length of time that you want to pay it back.

For other purchases, you have other options. For instance, you could use your credit card. Of course, this should be done if you can pay the balance off as quickly as possible or if, by any chance, the interest is at 0%. You can also take out a personal loan. These require a great credit score and usually have fixed interest, but you can use them for many different purchases, such as home renovations. At times, it might also require collateral, which means you have to put something where if you can't pay the loan back, they will take it from you, for example, a car.

Depending on what you are buying, the merchant might offer an installment plan where you pay for the purchase over several months. These are usually quicker to get approved, but you still need to have a good credit score. They obviously come with interest when you pay them back.

The Different Ways You Can Save for College

College is important for your future. Nowadays, while there are alternatives, people who go to college usually earn more throughout their lives. However, it's expensive, and if you haven't been saving, it can become difficult to pay for it. Although there are many different ways that you can pay for your college expenses. The examples I will give below are exclusive to the US, but most countries have similar options available.

The first one that comes to mind is the 529 Education Savings Plan. This is a state-sponsored investment account that helps save for college expenses. Any money in here can be invested in many different investment vehicles, such as mutual funds or ETFs. But it gets better: any earnings from this are not taxed, unlike other investment accounts. However, you can only use these funds for anything related to education, such as the cost of tuition, transportation to college, or educational materials. In fact, there are high penalties if you use it for anything else but education-related things and your portfolio is usually a lot more limited than other investment accounts.

Another savings account you can use for your education is the Coverdell Education Savings Account. Usually, your parents have to open these because they are custodial accounts before you are 18 years old. Like the 529, you don't pay taxes on earnings, but your parents have to have a low annual income to apply for it, and they can only contribute $2,000 per year.

Another option is scholarships, grants, or work-study programs. Before talking more about it, you can visit studentaid.gov to check all the options for grants, scholarships, and other financial aid for your education.

Let's start with grants. These are financial aids that don't need to be paid back unless you withdraw from school. The

Department of Education has many different grants that can help students pay for their education. Some of them are the Federal Pell Grants, the Federal Supplemental Education Opportunity Grants, and the Teacher Education Assistance for College and Higher Education. While eligibility changes, grants are only given to students who actually need financial aid to pay for their tuition.

Scholarships are offered by private and nonprofit organizations to help students pay for their education. Eligibility depends on many factors, such as talent or academic merit, but some are also based on financial need. Each scholarship has its own requirements, but a quick online search will give you all the websites you can visit to check on particular scholarships.

Work-study jobs are programs that allow you to earn money that you can then use to pay for your education. Usually, this work is part-time, so you can attend your education. While you can earn more than the minimum wage, this is not guaranteed. What you get from these work-study jobs depends on your level of financial need, the funding level of the organization, and when you apply for them.

Alternatively, you can also apply for a loan to pay for your education, but as you already know, this has to be paid back with interest, so it's important that you plan everything properly before doing it.

Big purchases and paying for college are things that might seem daunting, but they are part of life, and we need to go through them. In fact, with enough planning, they are not so hard to achieve. There are many different things that you can do and many different strategies that you can follow to reach these goals faster.

In the next and last chapter, I will talk about retirement, how to plan for long-term financial goals, explore retirement saving options that you can start right away, and the different strategies available.

CHAPTER 10

RETIREMENT

> *Retirement from work, but not from life.*
>
> — *M.K. Soni*

Y es, I know it's a long way until you retire; after all, you haven't even started to work, right? However, planning for retirement starts right now. In this last chapter, I'll be talking about retirement plans and the many different strategies you have, as well as the benefits of starting to plan this early in life.

How to Start Planning for Retirement?

When it's time to retire, you have worked all your life for yourself and your family. Now, you want to spend some quality time with your family and do what makes you happy—if you've planned properly, of course.

A retirement plan simply means that you have followed the right steps to live a comfortable life when it's time to stop working. There's not a single formula to plan for retirement, but there are guidelines. A retirement plan is important because you will have a regular income after you stop working, but you are also ready for any emergency and prepared to live a long, healthy life.

You have many investment options that will allow you to properly plan for when you retire. But like all kinds of investing, there are some with higher risks and higher rewards and others that help you protect your wealth. Let's take a look at the most common ones.

The Different Retirement Options

Before I get into the different retirement options, the examples I'm going to talk about below are specific to the US, but other countries have similar options available. The two most common retirement investment options are 401(k)s and IRAs. A 401(k) is a retirement savings plan that you often get through your employer, and it has tax advantages for you. When you are working, your employer will offer you a 401(k) that you have to sign up for if you want, and here, you are agreeing to give a percentage of your monthly income to your 401(k) savings plan, which is just like an investment account. Then, your employer usually matches what you have contributed. While you don't have all the options you'd have in your personal investment account, you can still pick from several investment options, but these are usually mutual funds because they are safer. In a traditional 401(k), any contributions you make are pre-taxed, which essentially means that you are not taxed on them now but will be when you eventually withdraw the money in your retirement. A Roth 401(k) works the same way, but it's after-tax, which means that your contributions are taxed right away but not when you withdraw the money in your retirement.

Then, you also have an Individual Retirement Account or IRA. This type of account also has tax benefits like a 401(k), and you can also contribute with pre- or after-tax money. This is a long-term savings account that works similarly to a 401(k), but it's not done through your employer. This is what self-employed workers use more often, and you can open it through your bank or even a brokerage. Here, you have four different types of IRAs: the traditional, Roth, Simplified Employee Pension (SEP), and Savings Incentive Match Plan for Employees (SIMPLE).

The differences between them have to do with the contribution limits. For instance, with a traditional IRA and a Roth IRA, you can contribute a maximum of $6,500 or $7,500 if you are 50 years old or older (however, these limits change every year). With a SEP, you can contribute a maximum of $65,000 or the lesser of 25%, and with a SIMPLE retirement account, you can contribute a maximum of $15,500 or $19,000 if you are 50 years old or older.

CONCLUSION

T hat's it! That's all you need to know to start your financial journey on the right foot and prepare for what's coming. I know, at times, it might seem a little overwhelming, but once you know how things are done and you allow yourself to create routines, everything becomes a lot easier.

Starting with the basics and understanding what money is and how to make money is fundamental. A good foundation will allow you to prosper in all the other areas of your personal finances. When it comes to making money, there are many different ways you can do it as a teenager, as you have seen in Chapter 2. Just pick whatever you are most comfortable doing or something that you believe you will be doing in the future. Gaining experience at this stage of your life will make it easier for you in the future. If you can, open a bank account (if you don't already have one) since understanding the basics here and how you can manage your account will make you more comfortable with these services. Understanding the two basic accounts—checking accounts and savings—will allow you to not only get paid but also grow your money effectively. Nowadays, everything is gamified, and bank accounts are no exception. With mobile and internet banking, it is a lot easier to understand what you are doing.

I cannot emphasize this enough: budgeting allows you to reach your financial goals, and you should make it a habit.

Regardless of the type of budgeting you follow, it's important to have one so you have your finances under control at all times. The more you know and the more you are in control, the better purchasing decisions you will make. This brings us to the different techniques when it comes to purchasing goods or services: practicing smart shopping and comparing prices can save you a lot of money in the long run and is one of those things that you want to have in your routine. Credit, credit cards, and debt can all sound scary, but as you've seen, credit can actually help you with your finances as long as you keep it under control. It can build your credit score and allow you more opportunities.

While savings are important, so is investing. In fact, investing, when done properly, can increase your wealth exponentially. Having savings goals is important, but having investment goals is also crucial so you can create a good financial foundation and be prepared for any financial emergencies that might come your way. Preparedness is everything. And don't forget compound interest, which can exponentially increase the value of your savings and investments even without adding any more money to them.

You might never have associated insurance with money or savings, but as we've seen in Chapter 8, it can be a great protection for your wealth, yourself, and your family. There are all types of insurance, such as health or auto, and while some are mandatory, others are recommended. This is especially true for health insurance in the US since these are mostly not covered by the government, and any minor medical emergency can become very expensive. It's important that you know how to evaluate insurance policies and coverage so you know you are properly protected, but you can also save money.

There's always a point in our lives where we have to make big purchases or have big expenses, such as purchasing a car, a home, or paying for our education. It's crucial that you plan properly and in advance, know how to evaluate your options, and explore the different strategies on how to save for these big expenses. Lastly, retirement might seem very far away, but we've seen the importance of starting early. This is probably the longest-term financial goal you will have, but even at your age, there are things that you can do to start planning for it.

However, I believe the most important thing you can do is apply the knowledge you have acquired in this book on a daily basis. There are many concepts here that might take a while for you to make a habit of, but with practice, everything is possible. Taking control of your financial future is something that many of us adults didn't have the chance to do, mainly because we didn't have the knowledge, but you do. If you apply everything you've learned in this book, you will not only have total control of your finances, but you will also live a stress-free life.

FINANCIAL LITERACY
FOR YOUNG ADULTS

*End Your Money Problems and
Reach Financial Independence at a
Young Age with Brilliant Budgeting,
Profitable Investing and Smart
Money Management*

EMILY CARTER

INTRODUCTION

"I believe that through knowledge and discipline, financial peace is possible for all of us."

— Dave Ramsey.

Y ou, too, can have it all – true, it sounds like a cliché from a commercial! But really, do you think you have what it takes to have it all?

I have been thinking a lot about how to begin this introduction, and I discovered that honesty always works best. So, I'm going to be honest with you. I am someone who has spent a lot of time, especially during my young adult years not really knowing how to handle finances. I was constantly struggling and reading books on the topic, but it seemed like something was missing.

Then I realized what that something was – I kept trying to blindly follow everyone else's experiences and how they handled money instead of finding a way that would work for me. Granted, it took me a little longer than expected to reach this point, but right after I did, I realized that everything I've ever learned about finances is finally making sense.

So, I began working – I did my best, invested, made safe (and a little risky) financial choices, and came up with multiple income sources. It sounds like a dream, doesn't it? Well, in the middle of it all, I found that I was losing my balance. It's not my actual balance (I can keep that), but my work-life balance. Suddenly, it felt like I was right there where I started. It was like I did a full circle and returned to the beginning. I felt discouraged and, again, thought that I didn't know where to begin. That's when something in my mind just clicked.

Financial literacy doesn't require a background in algebra or business – it requires a strong mindset and determination. It requires a little bit of persistence and some strategies, so you know you're making the logical financial steps. Once I implemented this behavior into my life, everything started making sense once more.

The beauty of finance is that you learn things about the world and society, but mostly yourself, with each passing day. It is also about gaining experience in what matters most to you.

The thing is, not a lot of people believe this. And I understand where you're coming from. As a young adult, you are currently at a crossroads – you want to achieve as much as you can in life. You know you can accomplish a lot, but you are also baffled by all the options out there, and the more options you have, the more confused you get. It seems like you cannot find the proper balance, and even if you do, you still have this overwhelming feeling that you're doing something wrong.

Well, I am here to tell you that all's well that ends well. You do not need to panic anymore or feel like you're letting yourself down because, through this book, you will learn all there is to know about finances. As you go through this book, you will notice that financial literacy includes a lot of different aspects, such as interest rates, pensions, loans, etc. To make things as clear and concise for you, I have added plenty of examples – after all, we all learn through examples in life, right?

You are embarking on a journey that will lead you straight to the gates of financial independence and security. Through it, you will learn about recognizing the importance of saving and spending, how to earn money, identify good and bad debt, and how to plan ahead. Even if a part of you thinks that you cannot learn all of this, I can assure you that after you read this book, you will emerge as a new, improved, and financially literate you.

So don't be afraid to turn the first page! I know there is at least a little excitement within you, just waiting to burst into flames. That will happen as soon as you learn everything I've outlined in these pages.

Forget everything you've seen until now. This book will provide you with a bullet-proof way of understanding money, looking at money, and handling money.

From one financial sprout to another – you got this!

CHAPTER 1

MINDSET

*"Make sure you have financial intelligence...
I don't care if you have money, or you don't have
money... you need to go, and study
finance no matter what."*

— Daymond John

T he most difficult thing you will encounter on your way to financial independence and success is getting into the right mindset. Up until this point in your life, you have probably relied on your parents or guardians to give you the financial stability you need. But the wheel never stops turning, our caregivers grow old, and we are the ones responsible for our own faith.

Picture this scenario – you finish high school; you go to college (or any other educational institution) and it is time for you to become an independent person. All of which sounds great – having the liberty to be who you want to be and do what you want to do, but one thing is constantly on your mind – *what about your finances?*

Whether you know that this stage in your life is fast approaching, or you've already reached it, learning how to get into the right financial mindset takes time. It is a challenging process, but it is also a rewarding one.

Financial literacy and mindset are not taught in schools. With that in mind, we can start our journey to educate you about the most important topics connected to finances – which will be the foundation of everything you do in the future.

Understanding the mindset required for financial success

A mindset is your belief and your attitude toward the world around you, how you perceive it, and how you respond to it. It is the glasses through which you see your life opportunities, challenges, and setbacks.

Cultivating a strong mindset starts with understanding how it affects your finances. A weak mindset will not result in financial success, but a strong one just might. Your mindset affects not only what you think but also what you do and how you make decisions. Do you approach finances with hesitation or determination? It's time to learn about the mindset you need for financial success.

Fixed or growing?

Nobody explains the difference between the fixed and the growth mindset better than Carol Dweck. She studies human motivation, and her research on this topic is exactly what you need to start your journey. In her study, the difference the two mindsets make in outcomes is extremely powerful. Some people succeed, and others don't (depending on their mindset). She explains how your view of yourself determines everything in life.

If you believe you are born with a specific set of qualities and think they cannot change, then you have a fixed mindset. The opposite of that is learning from your mistakes. In her words, "The hand you're dealt with in life is just the starting point for development." That's what a growth mindset looks like - and it is exactly what you need to begin your journey to financial stability, literacy, and independence.

Having a growth mindset means focusing on the most important aspects of becoming more successful and independent. By accepting this approach, you will be able to shift, learn, and progress every single time. This is exactly what you need to fight (or go with) the ever-changing currents of money. It is what will help you grow and re-discover your powers over and over again.

With that in mind, here are the most important financial aspects where you need to put your growth mindset to use if you want to achieve financial success.

Financial challenges

These are something all of us have had at some point in life. However, when you come face to face with financial challenges, it is crucial to know how to deal with them head-on. Setbacks in life happen – that's when you return to the previous point. A fixed mindset will lead you to defeat and constant fear, despair, and helplessness. Contrary to that, the growth mindset will enable you to see that current situation as an opportunity for growth and development.

Financial Education

As much as you have avoided this in the past, it is time to face the fact – financial education is a must. Learning about finances is a long-term process, one you should invest in every time you can. By continuously expanding your financial knowledge, you invest in yourself and your ability to tackle finances successfully.

Financial decisions

Another aspect where your mindset plays an important role is that a strong growth mindset can help you approach financial decisions with confidence, while a fixed mindset will keep whispering in your ear that you're making a mistake. If you have a fixed mindset, that does not mean you're fixed in one place. You can always switch to the growth mindset, no matter how long it takes. Accepting the fact that you get a valuable learning experience each time you make a financial decision is a step in the right direction.

Financial resilience

As I mentioned earlier, financial setbacks happen – but that doesn't mean you should think it is the end of the world. That leads us to the final point – financial resilience. Investing wisely, saving wisely, and having enough to weather the financial storms that may come your way is essential. A strong mindset can help you remain focused on achieving your goals. Once you have a clear roadmap, it can help you overcome challenging situations.

Developing a long-term perspective

The growth mindset may seem like an unattainable goal at this point. The reality is that anyone can reach it. There are a few practices you should consider on your way to shift your mindset entirely, and the first one is developing a long-term perspective. By doing so, you will start looking at your status quo objectively and working toward a better financial tomorrow.

Developing a long-term perspective is a process that encompasses the following steps:

1. Evaluate your current situation

When you are creating a long-term perspective about your finances, you need to look at your current financial position. This includes your cash flow, net worth, liabilities, expenses, assets, income, and credit score. Once you gather and organize the information, see how much you save, spend, and invest. By tracking your movements, you can identify your weaknesses and strengths and even issues you need to address in the future.

2. Write down clear goals

Having a long-term objective is a crucial part of the process, but you need to be clear and concise about it. Every one of us wants to achieve something with the money we make, and if you are honest with yourself, you will get the most specific answer out of you. Be specific and write down a clear goal. For example – instead of saying, "I want to save money," say, "I want to save (a specific amount) for (a specific purpose) in (a specific timeframe)." For example, "I want to save $20,000 for a down payment on a house in two years."

3. Develop a strategy

The next step is to take action. If you want to achieve your financial goals, it is only logical that you develop a strategy that will bring you closer to your objectives with each passing day. Consider a few options, check how much you need to invest, spend, and save. Then, consider whether you are willing to take some risks. Create a timeline for each goal and track your progress regularly.

4. Review your assumptions

The long-term financial plan consists of estimates and expectations too. You should base these assumptions on your current situation, goals, strategies, and objectives. Before proceeding in a new direction, ensure the premises are realistic and consistent with the current market climate. Incorporate a few different scenarios into the assumptions and closely monitor the outcomes. Doing this will help you identify all the opportunities, errors, gaps, and other aspects that may affect your long-term financial stability.

5. Adjust accordingly

A part of a growth mindset is learning how to bend to future outcomes – sometimes, you will need to take a different path from the one you initially set and accepting that fact helps you get closer to achieving your goals. You may find that some significant changes will amend your current trajectory, and it is important to consider them into the equation and constantly adjust accordingly. This can be anything from changes in your personal or professional life to changes in taxes, interest rates, and inflation. Always focus on being flexible and adapting to the new conditions with ease – as long as they still reflect your long-term goals.

6. Seek assistance

This is something you have already done by reading this book! Financial stability and success come from knowledge, and it is always a good idea to seek advice on this topic. By doing this, you can take some solid financial steps and implement everything you've learned to draft the perfect long-term financial plan. Getting some valuable information, insights, recommendations, and resources is what can take your entire planning to the next stage.

The compound effect

The Compound Effect is a book by Darren Hardy that has significantly changed the way I view and approach finances. The core of this book lies in taking small actions that align with your long-term goals. It focuses on always taking full responsibility for what happens to you and underlines the importance of measuring something before you start changing it.

Let's talk about this a bit. Why is this book so important that we are discussing it here?

There's a thin line between your mindset and what you achieve. To that extent, what you believe in is what you achieve. Think of it as the ultimate power of self-observation. It is about having a real conversation with yourself. Because the compound effect is a system that is running your life, whether you are aware of it or not, this goes unnoticed in most people's lives.

But the reality of the situation is that you are your own creator. You are in charge of your own life, and the sooner you realize that; the sooner you can take some steps to create a better, financially successful version of yourself.

Making the right decision is something you choose every day, from when you wake up to when you go back to sleep. These small decisions you make, the small steps you take – all of them shape your destiny – who you are and who you will become. To implement it into the business and finances aspect of your life, you create a small operating system based on your abilities, the funds available to you at the moment, and your goals. Making a success scheme is only the beginning. Your progress may not be visible to you, but once you reach the first, second, or even third milestone and look back on what you've created, you will see that your desire to live an extraordinary life filled with abundance and richness is happening.

The compound effect is a strategy through which you accumulate a certain amount of wealth by making some small, almost insignificant steps every day. Through time, if you stay consistent and make small choices that benefit you, you end up reaping the fruits of your labour - financial success.

Picture this - what would happen if you made a scheme as mentioned just now, and be 1% better, or give 1% more every day? What would happen to you already in one year? On the contrary, what would happen if you gave 1% less and less with each passing day?

Allow me to show the math: If you improve yourself by 1% every single day for 365 days (one year) in a row, you will end up being 37.8 times better than you were when you started. That is a 3780% increase! And let me tell you, that's a lot. On the contrary, if you were to be 1% worse or less each passing day, after a year you would end up being only 3% of what you were when you started.

Here's a very simple real-life example - with a physical workout. When you want to get better or give a little bit more every day in terms of exercising, you will not see the difference immediately (of course, nobody does). However, if you try to push yourself each day - with one more push-up, or one more lunge, or deadlift, by the time one year has passed, you will be unrecognizable.

The thing is, you will also be unrecognizable a year from now if you give less and less every day. If you start doing less than you should, and ultimately you quit working out, the results will be more than evident. Actually, they will be more than evident either way. What's left of you is to discover which way you will go.

The compound effect is best described this way. No matter how much you give, as long as it is more, it piles up on top of one another and multiplies until you reach a point where you have an abundance to enjoy.

The basics of the compound effect are in the growth mindset. As long as you adhere to that and to the points we have gone over in this chapter, there is no way to remain in the same situation you are in right now. At all times, remember that even the smallest actions you take, the ones you think are the least significant to your being and your professional life, matter a lot.

I can only hope that you have gained some insight into what you need to start creating your financial independence today. To give you a little reminder, review the summary below.

What did you learn from this chapter?

- What is your mindset, and how it can help you achieve financial success?
- The difference between a fixed and a growth mindset.
- The most important financial aspects for success.
- How to develop a long-term perspective (and stick to it).
- What is the compound effect, and the beauty of incorporating it into your financial planning.

As we close this chapter and look into the future, you might still find yourself on the edge about "what's about to happen." Even if your mind wonders about whether the worst-case scenario will come true or not, this book is designed to put all your negative thoughts about it to rest. It is also intended to answer the easiest and most challenging questions you didn't think to ask.

In the next chapter, we will talk about how to prepare yourself for "rainy days."

CHAPTER 2

WEATHERING THE STORM - PREPARE YOUR EMERGENCY FUND

"Tough times never last, but tough people do."

— Robert H. Schuller

We only touched upon this topic in the previous chapter, so now it is time to open it and see what hides beneath the surface. No matter how young or financially inexperienced you are, you have probably noticed by now that everyone faces an economically difficult period at some point in their lives. The fundamental principle that can help you escape it (should you face it yourself) is to remain calm, collected, and ready to take action. Yes, being financially unstable can indeed make you feel overwhelmed and even make you panic at times, but it is essential to let go of that so you can focus on what you can control – and ultimately change. These difficult times have always been temporary, and as the quote at the beginning of this chapter says – only tough people last. So, let's see what you can do to make the most out of this situation.

Now, you are going to learn all about planning. It is not just about working hard to achieve your goals – it is about being smart about them, determined about what you want, and giving yourself the time to turn around any financial situation you stumble into.

The importance of emergency funds and their role in financial security

Life has always been filled with surprises, and if there is one thing you can learn from, you should always have a "secret stash." What does that mean? The importance of having an emergency fund is often overlooked, but if you want optimal financial well-being, it is a must. It is kind of like a safety net, something that will keep you from falling on the ground and spiralling down about what you're going to do now. Having financial security gives you peace of mind.

So, what is an emergency fund?

Life is unpredictable, and everything can change in the blink of an eye. Of course, no need to get into a worst-case scenario right now, but you probably see where I'm going with this. Unforeseen expenses happen all the time. When these things happen, you must be prepared – this is when the emergency fund kicks in.

The emergency fund represents a stash of money you have put aside for emergencies and unexpected events. This indicates that you are safe no matter what happens to you, even when life throws you the biggest curveballs.

Why is the emergency fund so important?

There are a few reasons why having an emergency fund is so important:

- You are financially secure in case of an emergency.

- You are protected in case of a reduction in income or loss of a job.

- You can cover all sorts of expenses (whether it is medical bills, car bills, home repairs, or anything else).

- You get to be independent and confident in your financial choices.

- You avoid getting into debt.

- You can support both yourself and a loved one, a relative, or a friend.

- You have the opportunity to seize an unexpected investment or business opportunity.

- You are flexible and able to handle any disruptions in income.

- You are prepared for anything that comes your way – whether it is to achieve your future aspirations or experience some sort of an accident.

How to build an emergency fund?

All this talk about having an emergency fund made you think – how can you create your own fund? Take a look at the steps below.

1. Set a goal – The goal-setting part is crucial because you cannot create an emergency fund without it. To have a good financial backup plan, first, you need to choose how much you want to save. Many experts on this subject have said that a stash of three to six months of living expenses is an average amount. This includes rent, bills, groceries, and every other necessary expense.

   But this is not always the case, so you need to take a look at your unique current situation. You can start creating a target based on your circumstances and comfort level.

You might end up having to save less than you expected yet still have enough to call your savings an emergency fund. Just remember, the goal is to cover your basic needs if necessary.

2. Automating your savings – having a goal is one thing, but automating your savings is probably the best way to achieve that goal. When you view savings as substantial as paying your bills or buying groceries for the month, you will save the money you want much faster than expected. If possible, you can set up automatic transfers from your paycheck every month.

   It is the beauty of the "set it and forget it" approach. With little to no effort, you will create an incredible emergency fund. It can be a percentage of your paycheck, a fixed amount – anything you like – as long as it gets you started.

3. Cut back on expenses – and save the money instead. Creating an emergency fund requires a lot of discipline. It takes dedication, effort, and determination. You should be willing to change your spending habits. When you take a closer look at what you are spending on a weekly or monthly basis – make a detailed view of it, you can easily find something to cut back on. Some of the costs may be completely unnecessary, and even if they are the slightest changes, they can still make an impact.

   Don't fret over this one – no need to make drastic changes. It can be anything from changing your streaming service subscription, gym membership, anything, really! Notice the unnecessary expenses and take it from there.

4. Contribute more – this means that, at some point, you are bound to get some extra cash flow – it can be a tax

return, a bonus from work, or an extra project you've taken on. Take these funds and add them to your emergency fund. The extra contribution you make will go a long way when needed.

The reality is that you don't really need the money at the moment, so why not save it? It is still there, and you can still reach it anytime you want. Doing this adds an extra layer of financial safety to your life. Also, it gives you the opportunity to reach your emergency fund goals a lot faster.

While I talked about emergency fund being the foundation of your financial security, another thing you have probably already heard of might have already come to your mind - insurance. That is good, since insurance is an incredibly important part of financial security too. But what do you think of when you think of insurance? Do you imagine some sort of a safety net? Or do you believe it has something to do with life insurance, car insurance, etc? You are right either way. Before we move on to understanding financial risks, let's talk a bit about insurance.

Insurances

Sometimes, life happens, and this is the sole reason why people turn to insurance. We are not powerful against the grand forces, and unexpected things can happen at any turn. When, and if this happens, you need to know that you have something to fall back on. That's where the insurance kicks in.

So far, the word insurance is something you have probably associated with your parents or guardians, and you thought it was a "grown-up" topic. However, since you are entering your early adult years, you need to immediately focus on it so you can build a safer financial future on top of it.

There is a certain importance to having insurance in your life, and being insured is a part of being an adult. As an inexperienced party, it is okay to wonder where to begin. I know that insurance is not the most thrilling subject to talk about, but you should always have something to fall back on. While there are different types of insurance, some of them are very common, and an advised choice for young adults. This is where things get interesting. The types of insurance vary, and the ones below are ones you should strongly consider having.

1. Health insurance - this should be on the top of your list. If we take America into consideration, most people there need insurance to afford healthcare. Do your research so you can choose the right option for yourself. Why is this important? Because it will be the first thing you fall back on if you come face to face with medical debt. Fun fact - a lot of people in America get health insurance through their employer or their spouse's employer - and these people usually don't need extra insurance. Another fun fact - you can stay on your parents' health insurance up until the age of 26.

2. Auto insurance - this is for all of you who own a car. Even a small fender bender can cost a lot, and having auto insurance will ensure you have all the potential damage to the vehicle and bodily harm covered. The auto insurance varies from one model to the next, as well as the living location, your age, your credit score, and your driving record. You will need this all throughout your life, up until the point you stop driving a car.

3. Renters insurance - in case you are renting out an apartment, consider renters insurance. If you live by yourself or on a college campus - you need renters insurance. Just like with auto insurance, this also varies

depending on the location, the coverage amount, and the type of home, but it is usually of a very low cost. In turn, it covers the replacement of personal property in case of an unwelcoming situation, and a temporary living place if you are unable to live in the home you've rented.

4. Disability insurance - this is something that will provide you with insurance in case you are unable to work. Relying on a steady paycheck or working toward something more, something you've created yourself can take a toll on your overall health. In any case, you don't know what the future has in store for you, and the disability insurance is there in case something happens to you.

5. Life insurance - what you've probably heard the most - in movies, in series, in real life - life insurance is the talk of the town, every time. The reason why this is happening is because at some point in life, someone else may rely on your income for their financial well-being. Since life insurance is so common, it is cheap, and the right policy depends on your overall financial situation. How much you pay, how much risk you pose, and what type of policy you get will determine the coverage. You will stop needing it when your dependents no longer rely on you for financial support.

6. Homeowners insurance - as soon as you become a homeowner, you will need to get homeowners insurance because it covers anything from your personal belongings to the structure itself, to liability if someone is injured on your property. The homeowner's insurance depends on the location, size, and age of the building. For example, if you live in an area that is more prone to wildlife or tornados, you might need more premium insurance. As soon as you stop being a homeowner

and sell your home, you will stop needing this type of insurance too.

7. Pet insurance - last but not least, this is the kind of insurance that you will probably consider - but it has never crossed your mind until now. Being a young adult, you might have a pet by your side, and whatever that may be (a dog, a cat, a parrot) you need to insure them too - after all, they are sort of your property, right? Should anything happen to them, you should be prepared. From a routine vaccination and vet visits to urgent surgery, this type of insurance will cover up to 90% of your bills.

Considering insurance before you move on to understanding and managing financial risks is what will help you create a more solid plan. Now let's talk about risks!

Understanding and managing financial risks

Becoming a part of modern financial society means knowing what risk and risk management mean. This knowledge can enable you to develop resilience when times get tough.

In its broader terms, a financial risk represents the possibility of losing money on an investment. The results can be minor or major losses depending on the risk. This casts such a wide net that it serves both businesses and individuals. The dangers that may come with a financial risk are mostly related to odds. If this happens, you may be unable to satisfy your most basic needs.

While there are financial risks for businesses, governments, and markets, there are also individual financial risks – which will be the central point of our learning.

Everything from highly speculative investments to taking days off of work without a particular purpose may be a financial risk for you. As you go deeper into the topic of finances when reading this book, you will notice one thing – you are always 100% responsible for your own actions – nobody else can take responsibility for you. That is why, every time you take a step, you need to assess the risks and the potential consequences.

The dangers of financial risk may be beyond our control sometimes. How can that happen? Depending on where you have put your focus of attention, three main things can "go wrong."

1. If you are dealing with assets and market liquidity happens, you can either be at a loss or not able to sell or purchase something at a reasonable rate – proceeding with that kind of transaction may only result in a loss.

2. You may be at a loss of funding. When you are employed, things can change in the blink of an eye. Nobody is ever really safe. Sometimes, the company you work for may be forced to cut down on its spending because it doesn't have enough capital to pay off everybody.

3. Which leads us to the third thing - accidents. These things are by far the most out of your control, and they can come in various forms - personal accidents, or any other type of accident that may prevent you from being a fully functional part of the workforce may result in loss of cash flow.

Thankfully, while some things are out of your control, others aren't. Your finances can undergo a strategy where you can always be prepared for the unexpected. It is time to learn the basic methods of risk management. Their beauty is that you can apply them to every aspect of your life (even though we're only talking about finances here.) In the long run, these can help you apply yourself much better in financial situations and always come out on top.

Think of personal financial risk management as an invisible obstacle you need to be prepared for, should it become visible at some point in your life. Because it can be quite challenging to overcome once you come face to face with it, it is better to come prepared, right? Before you go into actual strategies that can help you make the most out of your risk management, let's talk a little bit about why you are doing it in the first place.

You're doing it for financial security. At the end of the day, everyone wants to be financially stable and independent. A part of risk management means focusing on having some backup. That is why it is important to focus on creating a solid emergency fund, having essential insurance, and learning how to deal with debt. Because you will know how to take better action once you realize where you're going with your strategy (what your end goal is).

To elaborate even more on the topic, here are some risk management strategies you can incorporate into your life:

1. Avoidance – avoid some financial activities that do not make you feel safe. For example, if you want to focus on your emergency fund and want to fill it up as fast as possible, why not remove some activity that doesn't contribute to the overall quality of your life? You can lower your alcohol or cigarette consumption and make a difference in more than one aspect of your life. You may feel better almost immediately.

2. Retention – this part is all about accepting a risk as it is given. Usually, this happens when you want to offset some larger risk down the road, such as health insurance for example. The more basic plan comes with a higher

deductible rate. In this case, you are at risk of paying more from your pocket should any medical expenses arise, but what is the chance of that happening? As this is a unique situation for everybody, assess yours before you act accordingly.

3. Sharing – this happens when you share the risk with somebody (often an employer). For example, they will share premium health insurance with you, and both parties will participate in the insurance benefits. This comes from the logic that the more people share it, the more the insurance costs will come down. Some people find this to be in their best interest.

4. Transferring – for example, when you want to insure your car, the risk is transferred from the individual and the car (that's you) to the insurer. As soon as you decide to create and sign a contract with an insurance company, the document will clearly state that some conditions have to be met. In this case, when those conditions are not met, the insurer is the one who takes complete financial responsibility.

5. Prevention and reduction – there are many ways for you to try to minimize your losses. As you can see, this is a pretty extensive list, with prevention and reduction as the last point. This method will not completely eliminate the risk but will only minimize it. In this case, you accept the risk but are focused on containing the loss and preventing it from worsening. Spotting potential issues in your initial plan can help you minimize your losses – naturally, if you act fast.

Moving as far away as possible from debt means always being prepared with an emergency fund. As you noticed, in this chapter we elaborated on all kinds of safety nets you can turn to - and you realised that whatever you do - it is a smart move for your future.

What did you learn from this chapter?

- That even though difficult times never last, you still need to know how to weather the storm.
- What is an emergency fund, why it is crucial, and how to create it.
- You learned about the most common types of insurance and learned that you need it in every stage of your life.
- What is risk management?
- Why and how are you at a financial risk?
- How can you shield yourself from it?

Once you learn the importance of emergency funds and risk management, it is time to explore some more exciting topics! While this was incredibly important, the next few chapters will teach you exactly how to make your financial dream of stability come true. In the following chapter, we will dissect the topic of budgeting. I bet you can't wait for this one!

CHAPTER 3

BUDGETING AND SETTING FINANCIAL GOALS

"A budget tells us what we can't afford, but it doesn't keep us from buying it."

— William Feather.

The fundamental aspect of becoming a grown-up is learning how to make and manage finances. When reality hits, most young adults are baffled and still trying to decide which direction to proceed. What we learned is that, in some cases, young people take personal finance courses after graduating high school. This is an excellent starting point for all those who want to learn all about budgeting.

But when this is not the case, how can you possibly know how to manage your finances properly? You could try. However, it might feel like a part is missing, like you could do more and do better.

This chapter is all about that – the knowledge to manage money is one of the most powerful things you can learn. It is time to learn the basic financial rules that can help you build a stable and healthy financial future.

Fundamentals of budgeting

By now, you have probably already heard about the importance of budgeting. It is one of the most crucial aspects of gaining financial freedom, and for a good reason – budgeting can help you become more stable in your management and create better long-term financial stability.

Before we delve any deeper, let's start with the most basic use – what is budgeting, and why do we use it? Budgeting is a known financial tool that can help you determine how much you spend daily, weekly or monthly vs how much you earn. People use budgeting as an approach to set realistic financial goals. It is the reason why everyone uses it – by budgeting, you can evaluate exactly how you spend and save your money and whether that aligns with your priorities or not.

When you start your budgeting, it is essential to realize that there are different budgeting methods, and after looking into these types, you should choose one that works best for you. Your budgeting success depends on finding an approach that works specifically for you. With that in mind, here are the three most common types of budgeting:

1. Traditional budgeting

This approach organizes spending into categories based on their expense type (fixed or variable expense*) and allows for a certain amount of money for each category. For example, when you have your fixed expenses ready, you make a plan for how much to spend on your variables depending on the day-to-day needs. Once you reach your limit, either put the rest in your savings account or simply stop spending for that month.

Fixed expenses are the ones that stay the same every month and do not change, such as rent, property taxes, loan payments, insurance, etc. Variable expenses are those that change from one month to the next, and these include groceries, utilities, entertainment, clothing, travel, commuting, etc.

2. Reverse budgeting

This type of budgeting is also known as "paying yourself first" because it prioritizes savings above all else. Instead of focusing on your spending, you focus on allocating the money that is at the top of your priority list and then go down the list. For example, if your goal is to save a certain amount of money and set your monthly savings to reach it, you do that first. Then, you turn to your fixed expenses and, finally, to your variable expenses. If you happen to run out of money somewhere along the way, revisit your plan to make the necessary adjustments – after all, you can't allow yourself to run out of money entirely, right?

3. Zero-based budgeting

This type seems like a pretty reasonable approach to many (especially those who are new to the subject of financial stability). Zero-based budgeting means allocating all of your income to specific functions – expenses, savings, donations, debt, and ensuring nothing is left before your next monthly income. With this system, you should reach "ground zero" by the time the month is up.

Practical steps for creating and sticking to a budget

The budgeting types may all seem easy on paper, but when it is time for you to start using them, things can easily go awry. That's why financial experts over the years have created a solid plan filled with practical steps – to help you create and stick to your budget. Taking the best steps and advice throughout the years helped create the best approach, as shown below. It will help you keep your finances in check, prepare for your future, and achieve all your financial goals.

- Track how much you spend. As a young adult, maybe tracking how much you spend on a night out is not the first thing on your mind. Well, it should be. In order to make a solid plan, you must understand where you spend your money first. Any type of tracking will do – a spreadsheet, a notebook, an app on your phone – as long as you manage to categorize your transactions. That will give you a sense of where you spend all the money you earn. There is no need to categorize them from the beginning; this is all about getting the bigger picture before you go into details.

- Prioritize your fixed expenses. You need to successfully manage your fixed expenses to improve your financial future and reach your goals. Whether it is a higher rent rate, a debt you need to pay off, or an insurance you want to maintain, setting aside enough to manage your fixed expenses will give you the stability you need. Instead of spending your hard-earned income on variable expenses of all kinds, taking care of your fixed expenses first gives you the freedom to focus on your goals.

- Set goals. These can be both short-term and long-term goals. Doing this is a great way to keep track of your financial success. It is a way for you to "keep your eyes on the prize." Remember, if you don't know where to begin, always start by writing things down – and start small. For example, you can dedicate an entire section to your short-term goals (let's say on a weekly basis) and work toward achieving them. Even the most minor practices, such as these, will significantly impact your financial stability and long-term success rate.

- Always go into detail. The best way to make a successful financial plan that will lead you to a happier future is to create a plan right down to the last detail. As such, this financial plan will help you assess your current position, identify what you want to achieve in the future and create a map of how to achieve them. You have all the freedom and control here. You can choose to go down any road – now that you know all the budgeting types, you just need to begin.

- The 50/30/20 budget. This is a very popular approach that many young people use. It has even helped me become a more responsible adult and is an easy concept to adhere to. It is all about splitting your income. Use 50% of your income to cover all the essentials (this includes both fixed and variable expenses such as rent and groceries). Use the 30% to buy yourself something you want that month (this part can be reserved for clothing, travel expenses, etc). Finally, use the last 20% to put aside – these will be your monthly savings. Once you start sticking to this simple rule of dividing your monthly income, you can easily budget your spending without removing some fun purchases you want to make that month.

- Dedicate a journal. As mentioned earlier (and it will be mentioned a few times more in this book.) Having a place where you keep all your notes and expenses is important, especially at the beginning of your budgeting journey. Doing this can help you organize your goals, your spending, your savings, and the time you dedicate to achieving your financial freedom. There is no right or wrong way of doing it. Just by writing things down, you are using a helpful method that will help you organize your life better.

- Keep your taxes in the back of your mind. Always keep your taxes in mind. The amount on your salary is not the exact amount that reaches your account. That is why a part of the planning process is using your monthly income after you've put aside the tax money. Do your research and see if you are eligible for tax deductions. If the answer is yes, you might reach some of your financial goals sooner than expected, (such as creating your emergency fund).

- There is also something called the envelope method. While you have probably not heard it until now, many people know it as a popular budgeting method that can help you control your expenses. The envelope method uses a few envelopes (of course). In each of these envelopes, you dedicate a certain amount of money you're allowed to spend for that particular cause. Take groceries as an example – it is something you spend money on every month, but the amount changes all the time. This way, you can make a partially fixed expense out of a variable expense, which is an excellent approach to managing your money. For one month, dedicate a certain amount of your income to groceries and put that money in the envelope. Sticking to the amount you've set aside for that purpose can help you avoid overspending. Doing this gives you a physical sense of the money, and you may take much better care of it by putting it to use every month.

- Control your savings by letting go of controlling them. In other words – automate your savings. This is another good practical tip that can help you start your budget. Since it was mentioned before, it means that it is a pretty solid step you can take. Instead of having your budgeting plan change every month, automate your savings by setting up automatic transfers. You have full control over the sum you want to put aside, and this money is automatically taken from your account when your paycheck arrives. It is mainly viewed as an effortless way of saving since you don't have to think over it – the money practically saves itself!

Setting achievable and realistic financial goals

As you read this chapter, the first thing you will probably stick to the most is the previous part, filled with practical steps on how to create a budget. But, when it comes to budgeting, you can't make a budget if you fail to include the financial goals you have. Starting to outline them means paving the way for your future - knowing how to set realistic and achievable goals means reaching financial maturity.

You've been trying so hard to achieve your financial goals. You've done everything and adhered to all the steps, some of you have even taken a side hustle to achieve your goals. However, when the end of the month comes, something is still missing – and that's usually the amount of money you were supposed to save.

In today's world, things like inflation and recession can be a solid excuse for why you can't save. You may even try to make an excuse by claiming that the above-mentioned practical steps don't work in real life. But we both know neither is the case.

Setting achievable and realistic goals is about wanting to make progress with your money – you're not just saying that; it is something you genuinely wish to achieve. Many people make the mistake of sticking to a certain financial approach without having any financial goals in the first place. So now, we are taking a step back and learning all there is to know about financial goals before going to the next chapter at full speed!

You probably set goals for every aspect of your life. The same should go for finances. Setting a financial goal means knowing what you want to do with your money (having a plan for it.) This goal makes you committed. But, if you want to achieve lifelong success, then you need to prioritize. That's where this book comes in handy! Your reality is this – a lot of things can influence what you think and how you set specific financial goals. They depend on your dreams for the future, your spending habits, your income, and how well you handle money. It takes a lot to handle your goals and make them as specific as possible. That's why you should look into the actionable steps below – I bet they will greatly help you.

1. Start by putting yourself as a priority. There is a reason why this is the first step of the process - you need to be calm, centered, and ready to take on the challenge that is your financial stability. When you decide the only person, you want to work on is yourself, everything else will start falling into place.

2. When you focus on your goals, writing them down is what will help you get a sense of them. There is something about putting things, "pen to paper" as they say that fully validates the intent of the goals - it makes them stronger, it makes them real, and it helps you stay committed.

Also, while you write down your goals, make them as specific as possible. One of the main reasons why people don't succeed in their quest to reach their goals is because their goals are not specific enough. Instead of being vague, be as specific as possible. For example, if you are looking to build up a good safety net of financials stored in the bank, don't say that to yourself – be specific! Write the exact amount you want to have in your savings account. That makes the goal measurable, too, not just specific. You can almost touch it. You can write them in your journal, on your phone, on a Post-it, on a piece of paper, etc., and take them anywhere you go. There is something about this that will make you work harder than before.

3. Make a deadline. Now, this may put a little bit of pressure on some of you who have been more than eager to reach your goals and be the boost you need from others. Either way, it is okay. As long as you approach this as a challenge you know you can overcome, you will eventually stop saying, "I will be one day," and will start saying, "I already began." A deadline will give you another dimension to make your financial goal setting feel more real.

4. Ensure yourself they are your goals, not someone else's. Sometimes, we all get influenced – by the people around us, society, tradition, and current standards of what is acceptable and what isn't. This can happen without you ever noticing it - so check the goals with yourself before you set them in stone. However difficult it may be, you need to be completely truthful to yourself as you write down the goals. Are these financial goals yours, or are you simply creating goals just to "catch up with the people around you?" If you are not in the same place as some people around you, that's okay. It doesn't mean that you are not in a good place if you're not there alongside them. Stay in your lane, and always ensure the goals you write down and set out to achieve are yours completely and uniquely.

5. Get a buddy. With that in mind, every person needs a little help regarding accountability. To take your entire financial planning a step further, you need to find a so-called accountability buddy. This could be anyone – a friend, a relative, your partner – anyone who can cheer you on your journey and check on you to see if you're still going on the right path. They can help you out whenever

times get tough. Also, you will immediately notice the difference in your journey. It means a lot to have someone stand by you, while you work on achieving your financial goals.

Budgeting is a process where you will keep going back and forth - but knowing that taking a step back doesn't mean retreating, but rather trying to look at the bigger picture is what this subject is all about. By determining your financial goals and taking the practical steps to achieve them you will create the foundation of your financial freedom.

What did you learn from this chapter?

- You learned what budgeting is.
- You discovered the three most common types of budgeting, each explaining how it can assist you in achieving your goals.
- Sticking to a budget takes a lot of practical steps – you learned the best ones, expanding your knowledge on managing money.
- You took a step back to collect yourself – learning what financial goals are, how to set them, and how to make them as realistic as possible so that you can achieve them.

Now, you know how to approach money to create and manage a budget. Before this chapter is over, remember this – it takes a lot to learn, and it takes a lot to practice, too, but nothing is far from your grasp! Hone your budgeting skills with time, and until that time passes, let's move on to the next chapter and talk about a topic called debt!

CHAPTER 4

GOOD AND BAD DEBT

"A man who does not plan long ahead will find trouble right at his door."

— Confucius.

E ven in ancient times, having a good financial plan was necessary. It seemed like everything revolved around making good decisions, especially when you needed to take a risk and do something for yourself. The thing is, sometimes that risk pays off, and sometimes it doesn't. As a result of these choices, you will enter into what we know today as good and bad debt.

Most people (specifically young adults) view debt as a bad term, but it is not necessarily one. Only a handful know how to handle themselves whenever they come face to face with debt. This chapter puts you in the middle of that handful – because you will learn everything there is to know about this term.

Defining good and bad debt

A debate over good and bad debt has been ongoing for ages. People have discussed it in person, online, anywhere they can. But not all seemed to have found a definite explanation for debts and why they differ. Also, people don't even use the terms correctly, making the matter all the more confusing.

The reality is that there is a distinct line between good and bad debt, and it is all about what it does for you in the long run. Since you are a young adult, it is time for you to enter what is considered the core of the finance world and learn all about good and bad debt. Learn how to define and differentiate them and how they impact your budget.

The defining line between good and bad debt is the list of consequences. Here's the difference you need to know:

- Good debt is something you can benefit from in your life overall. Even if you are in debt right now, the benefits will remain there once you pay it off.

- Bad debt is the exact opposite – this type of debt does not give you any long-term benefits whatsoever. In this case, all you're left with is debt.

After reading this, you might think that good and bad debt are two very distinct and clear situations. This is where the line gets all blurry. It can be confusing to differentiate the two.

The thing you need to consider here before you begin managing your debt is the difference between good and bad debt. Let's dive a little more into this concept before we proceed.

Take buying an appliance as an example. If you invest in a technology appliance, then you get to reap the benefits from it long after you've paid off your debt. But in this case, as soon as you purchase your appliance, its value decreases, so it's a thin line you're walking. The same applies when you're buying a car. The moment you buy the vehicle, its value starts to decrease, so it will not give you plenty of value in the long run.

This, however, is not the case with property. Buying a house or an apartment fluctuates in value, meaning a mortgage can be a good debt. The value of the property you've invested in may decrease or increase in the future.

Sounds a bit confusing. Let's get into the details.

Some examples of GOOD debt are the following:

Mortgage – for most, this one is probably the best debt you will ever encounter. Property always had and always will have value, and this is something that generally increases over time.

Student loans – these are mostly considered good debts. Getting your education and earning a degree increases your value as an individual in the future. It can be something you build upon and will give you great advancement in the job market. This means more opportunities and bigger chances of increasing your net worth. That's why student loans are considered a good debt.

Investments – the exception to this rule is if you invest in anything that might potentially increase in value in the future. This applies to, for example, businesses, ventures and collector items. However, even in these cases, there are certain risks, and you might get stuck in bad debt. You need to be extremely careful here.

Some examples of BAD debt are the following:

Personal loans – any type of personal, short-term loan used by people in case of an emergency – and they never give you something back. Their interest rates are extremely high, and getting a personal loan may mean paying back with an interest rate as high as 300%.

Credit card debt – no matter what you buy with your card, it is mostly considered a bad loan. This is because credit cards have the highest interest rates, and depending on the item you purchase, these rates can either double or triple.

Most auto loans – I have already explained what most car loans are – a bad debt. The value you get of the car in the end doesn't really match what you've paid in the first place.

Pawn shop loans – exchanging an item of value for cash is only familiar to those who have been strapped for cash at some point in their life. This is when the value may decrease, but as soon as you go back for it, its value may just increase to a point where you can't afford it anymore. It is the definition of a bad debt.

Let's explain this concept a little further. The good and bad debt are, of course, both debts, only with the former, while you get into debt, you have a certain way of getting out of it. With the bad debt - you're just in debt.

The defining line can become even more complex - let's say for example that you want to purchase a car. When you want to make this kind of a purchase (a larger one) you basically have two options - either you buy it with cash, or you buy it with financing. This is where things get interesting. When you buy your car with cash, all of your money will be tied to that particular purchase. But on the other hand, should you decide to buy it with financing, you only need so much to cover the down payment. So, you would take the financing and buy the car you want, but with the rest of your cash, you can invest the remaining amount, and even get a higher interest in that than the interest of your loan. By doing this, with the returns of the investments, you can get some help in paying back your initial loan. This is a good debt. In simpler terms - one you have a solid plan to get out of before you even take it.

Managing student loans and other common debts

You are a young adult, and this is probably something that would interest you the most right now. Taking care of your student debt (or some other common debts) is part of getting your finances in order. If you are just starting college or finishing college, or you have a debt you want to get rid of, it is understandable to want to know how to approach this accurately. Even if you plan to take out a student loan, the right strategies are key.

On the other hand, "putting all your eggs in one basket" as they say, is the bad kind of debt - one you should avoid as much as possible. The thing is, life happens, and sometimes, due to the challenges you are faced with, you may come face to face with bad debts, and in these situations, you should have detailed steps on how to get out of it. The following segment includes getting out of debt overall - a layout of tips that can help you rise above all the curveballs of life.

Managing student loans can be either tricky or easy business – depending on your point of view and the action steps you take. If you want to pay them off as soon as possible, here are some tips you can implement!

Make a plan.

Creating a plan that outlines exactly how you will manage your income and expenses is a great first step. If you have a student loan you need to repay, you should make a solid plan and track how much of your income can be allocated to the repayment every month. This will not only help you set aside a solid amount each month, but it will also prevent you from overspending elsewhere.

Instead of guessing or thinking of an approximate number, look into how many loans you have - that will give you the total amount of what you should repay.

Refinance and automate.

When you refinance your student loan, you consolidate the existing loans into one loan to get a lower interest rate. In the long run, this can help you reduce your interest rate significantly – and because of that, it has become an appealing option to many. Interest rates have been dropping over the years, and if you have a good credit score and no negative marks, then you have the golden chance to use this tip and demonstrate smart financial behaviour.

Knowing the loan terms can also help you budget accordingly, this can help you dedicate just the right amount from your income every month, and with a lower interest rate. From that point on, to make things a lot easier for you, you can automate your payments to make sure you pay on time, all the time.

Go through the most popular assistance programs.

The first section is the government - always there to help you out, especially in the case of federal student loans. With their help, you can manage your debt by enrolling in an assistance program. By being a borrower, you can check if you are eligible for these government programs before you make your decision. Many deferment and forbearance options can provide you with reduced monthly payments based on your income. Keep in mind that these only apply to federal student loans.

The second section is your employer – some companies offer assistance programs that are specifically created to help employees pay off student loans. The contributions they make and the help they offer vary from one company to another. For example, they can help you make payments on your loan, give you the option of access to refinancing, and even offer to fully repay the loan after you've worked there a certain amount of time (and showcased your skills). Whatever option they give out, it is usually something you can communicate with them – that's what makes these companies an attractive option for many young adults.

Start budgeting properly.

As a borrower*, there are many practical ways to implement proper budgeting if you want to manage your loans successfully. The most common approach people take is saving money. This is a practical solution, and it has helped reduce both student and other types of loans. It is the basis of doing proper budgeting with the money available to you. Each month, you can dedicate a certain amount to minimizing your loans or debts by focusing on saving money. Try doing one of the many things – using public transportation instead of a car while traveling to work, searching for discounts when purchasing something, and taking advantage of free or discounted resources available on your campus (when you are a student). With a lot of careful planning and taking advantage of all resources at hand, you can stay on top of your student loan payments.

*Borrower is someone who received a certain amount of money with the obligation to pay it back (most of the time with interest).

Remember, getting rid of your student loan is not unmanageable – all you need is a proactive and highly organized approach – and that's exactly what you will get here.

Strategies for debt repayment and avoiding excessive debt

As you grow, the student loan might not be the only debt you have. No person wants to have a debt, but these things may happen, most of the time, without you even noticing them. Some people believe that going into debt is completely out of their control, but nothing can be farther from the truth.

Even if you happen to go into bad debt, there is always a way out. Correct – it will take a lot of prioritizing, but the strategies you will learn here are ones you will follow for the rest of your life. It is in situations such as these that you will learn how to strategize and do everything in your power to achieve your goal - getting out of debt.

Avoiding excessive debt and the best strategies for debt repayment are as follows:

1. One of the most dangerous things that are closer than you think is credit cards. I mentioned them earlier in this chapter as a part of the bad debt, and I meant it. They create the illusion of being able to pay for something

when, in reality, you can't. If there is one good rule you can live by, it is this one – if you cannot afford it without a credit card, then you should probably refrain from buying it.

So, what's your strategy here? Open your wallet and check how many credit cards you have. Check your balance on each of them and write it down. See how many of these make you drag along debt and focus on them. Go down into specifics - how you will repay it, when, etc.

2. If you do have a credit card, try to limit its use and limit the amount of credit cards you have. The more credit cards you have, the more interest and payments you have to make. Doing this will minimize your chances of effectively and responsibly handling your cards. Instead of losing track of your expenses, have one card and keep track of everything.

    So, what's your strategy here? Once you've repaid the critical cards, go down to one or two cards that you will use. Add a limit to them, and only use them in cases of emergencies.

3. Build up that emergency fund we talked about before. Having a safety net is important; someone should tell you this and nudge you toward saving rather than having to experience it firsthand. Life throws you curveballs all the time. Literally, anything could happen – you could lose your job, you could sustain an injury that would prevent you from doing your job for a while, or anything unexpected may happen. This is when you should rely on the money you've saved rather than going into debt.

So, what's your strategy here? Paying off your debt was the first step, but the second is trying not to get into new debt by simply allocating your finances elsewhere - to your savings account. It is one of the smartest moves you'll ever make, creating that safety net I mentioned, instead of running into a bad situation once again.

4. Focus on what you need rather than what you want. Let's face it: every single one of us has needs and wants. But in this case, what separates you from a financially responsible adult is focusing on your wants rather than your needs. By tweaking and changing your perspective (and your spending habits), you can improve your finances and manage debt.

So, what's your strategy here? The emergency fund is exactly what I'm talking about in this case. Being a responsible adult means looking into the future. Another way you can practice this strategy is by investing your money - but more on that later on.

5. Budgeting may be difficult, but it is necessary. It is a way of tracking where your money goes in a month. You will also be able to see how much you have saved, how much you have spent (and where), and prioritize your debt, too. Think of tracking your finances as tracking your success – after a few months of doing good budgeting, you will immediately notice a difference.

So, what's your strategy here? As you can see, every strategy goes on top of one another - you start with paying off your debt, checking your cards, making a plan on how to repay it, saving for rainy days, investing, and now living on a budget. To some of you this may sound like a scary concept, but what's scarier - living on a budget or living with a debt? Calculate how much you need for the basic monthly expenses - you know what to do with the rest.

6. As luck would have it, you may get a pay increase. What to do with this unexpected cash influx? The answer to this question is simple – either put that money aside for rainy days or use it toward your debt management – either way, they are more than welcome!

So, what's your strategy here? This is the easiest (and the least probable) thing to happen to you, but if you're lucky enough, you might get that extra money - just enough to cover your monthly payments. This, along with all the other strategies I mentioned just now, can help you get rid of excessive debt and help you stay as far away from debt as possible.

What did you learn from this chapter?

- There is a difference between bad debt and good debt.
- Knowing what good and bad debt are will help you make better financial choices.
- Look into the options that can help you manage student and other common loans.
- Some incredible strategies to avoid and manage debt – lifelong knowledge on making the most out of your finances and current situation.

Navigating the financial terrain can be a challenge for many, especially when you are a young adult. But that should not stop you from going after what you want! Doing that will soon lead you to the next door you need to open and think about - credit cards and credit scores. With this in mind, we are turning the page together and walking straight into a room filled with useful information. It is time to start learning that everything you do counts.

CHAPTER 5

A NEW TERRAIN - CREDIT CARDS AND CREDIT SCORES

"Plastic is the money of our generation."

— Anthony T. Hincks

I t seems that, in the world of finances, every number counts. With that in mind, you need to know how to deal with what the world knows as a credit card and a credit score. In this chapter, you will learn that these two are very important parts of your journey to financial independence. Your future depends on the relationship you build with them, so read this chapter carefully.

How to use credit cards responsibly

It is of utmost importance to know how to use credit cards. Learning this can help you maintain your financial stability and can help you avoid debt overall. The thing is, not many people focus on the severity of the consequences of having a credit card, and they only focus on the perks. Don't get me wrong, there are many perks, but when you're young, and not financially literate, you have a higher chance of using the credit card in a way that will make you accumulate debt. Managing credit cards responsibly will be one of the main topics of this chapter. To understand how to do that you need a detailed guide - and I have made sure you have just the thing you need!

Understanding the concept of credit cards

Before going deep into the guide, you need to understand how credit cards work. In a way, it is sort of a way of borrowing money. Using that payment method constantly means you are constantly borrowing money from the issuer, while constantly agreeing to pay that amount back to them at a later stage.

1. Start with your financial status quo

To get a credit card you need to apply for one first. Before doing that, take a look at your current financial state. Take your expenses and your income into consideration and see if you have the means to repay the debts from the credit card you're about to make. By doing this, you will know whether you are financially stable enough to get a credit card. Also, from all the options you may come across, choose the one that will fit your needs and finances the most.

2. Choosing the credit card

Let's talk a little bit about that now, shall we? There is a plateau of different credit cards available, all of them ready to fit anyone's needs and lifestyle. Some of them offer small rewards such as cashback. Others offer incredibly low interest rates and travel perks. From all the options that may be in front of you, choose the one that has the most straightforward terms and conditions, the best annual fees, and the best interest rates.

3. Start budgeting

To successfully manage your finances, you need to set your budget - and know it on a monthly basis, including everything you put on your credit card. As you can notice, it all comes down to tracking your income and expenses at the same time so you can understand how much money you spend, and where. Take your necessities, your bills, and your savings into account. Include the credit card payments in your budget too. Making a budget means you should be able to cover all your expenses without going over it.

4. Paying your balance

Each month, you need to be able to pay your balance in full. This is one of the most important rules if you want to use your credit card responsibly. Avoiding interest rates is a must. Avoiding excessive debt is a must too. By paying your balance in full every month you maintain a good credit score. Set up the automatic payment we talked about in the earlier chapters and that way, you will never miss a deadline.

5. Check how much you spend

We all want something that is a little bit out of our grasp at the moment. This can be anything from fancier clothes to a luxury vacation. But, and this is important, you need to monitor how much you spend each month. Keeping track of your spending means that you will know how much you need to get through the month, bills and everything, leaving you just enough room to "wiggle" around. Note your spending patterns, identify any possible issue, and make adjustments to your spending as you go.

6. Refrain from spending too much on impulse

Having a credit card in your pocket seems like you have something you can just "swipe" any time you want something. The credit card looks like it can make all your dreams come true. However, lack of physical cash in your pocket can make you go into debt very easily. No matter how difficult it is, try to refrain from spending a lot of money.

7. Have a low credit utilization

The credit utilization means the percentage of available credit you're using at the moment. By keeping it low, preferably below 30%, you can maintain a good credit score. If it is high, then you have probably maxed out your credit cards, and you have stretched yourself too thin (financially).

8. Always check the fees

Fees are always there, embedded into the fine print of your credit card agreement. They vary and they can be late payment fees, balance transfer fees, annual fees, etc. As soon as you familiarize yourself with how your credit card works, you will be able to avoid any of those fees.

9. Use the rewards

And use them wisely! Every credit card nowadays comes with some kind of a reward - be it points, miles, cashback, or something else. I suggest you take full advantage of the reward payment programs, and benefit from your spending. But the line here is incredibly thin - try not to overspend just so you can earn a specific reward.

10. Check your statements

A part of being financially responsible is checking your payments regularly. Verify all the transactions you have made on a monthly basis and check if there are any unauthorized charges. This way, you can easily spot any fraudulent behavior and protect your credit score.

11. Credit history

This is something that you build over time, as a responsible credit card user. Such behavior may serve you in the future if you plan to apply for a loan or a mortgage. It is all about managing your credit in a responsible way - such as paying your bills on time, keeping your credit utilization low, etc.

12. Prepare for the worst-case scenario

All of us want to avoid this, but in case it happens, you should come prepared. Think about having a credit card with an available credit line. This can give you a safety net in case any unexpected expenses happen. But, in this case, keep in mind you should pay these off as soon as possible, as they come with a sky-high interest.

Understanding Credit Score

To further learn how to navigate through the field of finances, you need to know something about credit scores. For this particular topic, let's start from the very beginning.

The credit score consists of three digits that show whether you are an okay candidate for a credit to any creditors and lenders. The information that is gathered to create this number comes from your credit report. This number shows the lender everything they need to assess the risk of giving you money.

But how is the credit score actually created?

There are a few segments that play a particularly important role here. Here are the components of a credit score:

1. Your payment history - is about 35% of your overall credit score. By far the most valuable contributor to your credit score - it reflects whether you have submitted all your bills on time, and whether you have had any late payments.

2. Your credit utilization - is about 30% of your overall credit score. This represents the credit you are using at the moment compared to your total available credit. This is what I mentioned earlier - if you keep it below 30%, you have a good credit score.

3. Your credit history - is about 15% of your overall credit score. It shows the duration of time that you've been using credit. Generally, the older credit history is something that the lenders prefer.

4. Your type of credit - is about 10% of your credit score. When the lenders are viewing your information, they would prefer to see a mix of credit types, such as mortgages, installment loans, credit cards, etc. The variety in your credit portfolio can positively impact your overall credit score.

5. Your new credit - is about 10% of your credit score. For example, if you open a few new credit accounts in a short period of time, the lenders will assume you are in financial distress. This may lower your credit score.

After knowing what credit score is and what it consists of, it is time to turn to its importance. Below you will find a few reasons why credit scores are so important.

- Access to credit - a good credit score will open up a lot of doors for you - meaning new opportunities, including mortgages, credit cards, and loans. The lenders will assess the risk of lending you money.

- Interest rate - the credit score will affect the interest rate you receive on your credit cards and your loans. The higher credit score mostly means lower interest rates - which will save you some money over time.

- Premium insurance - the insurance companies nowadays use credit scores to determine the insurance for rent, home, and auto. The higher credit score may mean lower insurance premium, as it means lower risk.

- Rental applications - the property management companies as well as the landlords check the credit scores as a part of the application process. A good credit score may increase the chance of you being approved for rental housing.

- Job opportunities - even though this is not that common, some employers may review the credit score as a part of the job hiring process, especially for positions that require financial literacy. A good credit score may just get you the job you want!

- Services and utilities - the service providers and utility companies may check the credit score if you want to set up a new account with them. A good credit score may help you get lower deposit fees.

After this, you may ask yourself how can you get a good credit score, and maintain it? The first thing you need to do is pay your bills on time. By doing this, you maintain a good credit score. I cannot emphasize the importance of automatic payments here. Make sure to set that up and you won't have any worries.

Then, you may just want to try not to max out your credit cards. Constantly monitor your credit report and check for any errors or erratic behavior on your part. Avoid opening a lot of new credit accounts within a short period of time and try to have a mix of credit types to improve your overall score.

Tips for building and maintaining a good credit score

With credit score, as we move further deep into the chapter, you will notice that everything comes down to financial stability. No matter what your goal is - improving your score or establishing credit, here are a few tips that can help you achieve that. You are already familiar with some of them, while the others are brand new, but there's one thing they all have in common - they're incredibly helpful and will set you on the right path of financial independence!

- Always pay your bills on time. No matter what happens, try to be as consistent as you possibly can with your payments. The payment history you have is the most important thing about your credit score. So, making sure that all your bills are settled will help you avoid any negative impacts on your overall credit score.

- Keep the credit utilization low. Keeping the credit card balance to your credit limits means you are doing a good job. A high utilization ratio may have a negative impact on your overall credit score. To keep a healthy score, try to stay below 30%.

- Diversity is key. A diverse credit mix means a positive impact on your credit score. In this case, while you are maintaining that diversity, try not to overdo it. By that, I mean there is no need to open new credit accounts within a short period, especially if you can manage those you already have perfectly well.

- Try not to close old accounts. Why? Credit history is important, and it just may be the determining factor of your credit score. If you close the old credit accounts you will automatically shorten your credit history, thus lowering your overall score. Keep the accounts active and open, even if you don't use them frequently.

- Monitor your reports. Create a schedule where you review your credit report and make that as frequently as on a monthly basis. Check for any irregularities or errors, and should that happen, act accordingly. Your reports should always reflect accurate information.

- Limit your new credit inquiries. Every time you apply for new credit, there is a hard inquiry which is recorded on your credit report. In the future, this may lower your credit score. Limit the number of new credit inquiries, and try to apply for credit only when necessary. Also, when you apply for credit, try to be as selective as possible about the offers in front of you.

- Automatize your payments. Consider these the ultimate words of wisdom. If you miss a payment on any type of bill, then it may have a great impact on your credit score. By setting automatic payments, you will never have to worry about a payment deadline. This will help you avoid late fees and keep a straight payment record.

- The credit should be used responsibly. A responsible use of the credit you get means you will maintain a good credit score. Stay committed and borrow only as much as you can repay. You don't need a high balance on your credit card. The credit should only be used to help you wisely manage the finances instead of overspending.

- Consistency is important. Patience is important too. Creating and maintaining a good credit score takes time, effort, and patience. It takes consistent financial habits. To achieve your goal, you need to stay committed, and as time passes, you will be able to both achieve and maintain this.

- The help of a professional is always a good idea. If you feel like you cannot make it on your own here, but still want to do everything to improve your credit score, then you can always seek assistance from a financial advisor. They have the knowledge and experience to provide you with the guidance you need as well as the additional strategies to achieve the credit score you want.

How to obtain and review your credit report for accuracy

Now, we move on to the next step, which is reviewing your credit report for accuracy. Being "in good financial health" means knowing that all the information shown on your credit report is correct. The best way to help you get to the bottom of this is to follow a step-by-step guide, as shown below.

1. Start by requesting your credit report. You are entitled to one free credit report every 12 months. There is an authorized website called Annual Credit Report, where you can get it for free as mandated by federal law.

2. Select the reports. Once you are on the site, follow the instructions to fill in the request.

3. Verify your identity. In order to access your credit reports, you will need some personal information to confirm your identity. This usually includes anything from a social security number to a date of birth and current address. There may even be some security questions.

4. It is time to check your credit scores. To make sure you're thorough and have checked all the necessary information, pay close attention to the four main sectors - personal info, account info, inquiries, and public records. You already know what should be included in the personal info (your name, address, and other personal details), as well as the account info (your list of accounts, loans, credit cards, etc). In the section inquiries, check whether you have had any in the past period, and verify that the ones you have are from you. Finally, within the section public records, look for anything that may appear on your credit report - tax liens, foreclosures, and so on. Make sure everything is up to date.

5. Take action if you notice any discrepancies. You have the right to do that - process your dispute online, by phone, or via email. To support your statement, add the relevant documentation. Do a follow-up to ensure it is resolved.

6. Do this monitoring regularly. Make a habit out of it. Reviewing your credits at least once a year will help you maintain your credit score and take full control over your financial situation. You can even subscribe to some credit monitoring services that provide alerts any time the credit report changes.

These simple rules will do so much more for you than you imagine. As a young adult, someone who is just stepping into the shoes of a financially responsible person, you need to remember that it is all about having the correct and latest information. If that isn't the case, now you know how to act on it (and fast) and ultimately protect your financial stability.

Now let's talk a little bit about those plastic things we know as credit cards.

Borrowing money through credit cards has something called APR (Annual Percentage Rate). It plays a crucial role in borrowing money. To make a fully informed financial decision, you need to know how credit cards function too. Let's take a look at it together.

Types of credit card interest rates

As I just mentioned the APRs, here is what you need to know about the different types.

- Purchase APR - this is applied to any purchase you make with the credit card. You can even carry the balance from one month to the next, by not paying the statement balance in full, and get an interest charge on the purchase APR.

- Balance transfer APR - depending on the credit card you choose, you may receive a promotional balance transfer APR, which will allow you to transfer a balance from other credit cards at a decreased rate. But this usually only happens for a promotional period.

- Cash advance APR - any cash advances that involve withdrawing cash from an ATM usually have a higher interest rate than the purchases. The cash advance APR applies to these transactions.

Factors that affect credit card interest rates

Believe it or not, the interest rates vary due to several factors. When it comes to credit cards, these are the ones you should know:

- Your credit score - here is how the credit score and credit cards are connected. The one significantly influences the other. The ones that have higher credit scores usually have lower interest rates, and vice versa - all depending on the perceived risk.

- The market conditions - the credit card interest rates also change as the market current changes too. There are broad economic factors that play a crucial role in this, including market competition, and inflation.

- Type of credit card - this too plays a big role. Depending on the card you have, the interest rates, benefits, and features will vary.

- The limit of the credit card - last but not least, we have the spending limit. It represents the maximum amount of credit extended to the cardholder (you).

This last line might have confused you for a moment there, so this is why I am expounding on it too. Understanding the credit card limits can help you manage your spending better and maximize the efficiency of the credit card itself.

The initial credit limit is important. This is set up based on a few factors, such as your income, your existing debt (should you have any) and how worthy you are to receive credit. As time passes, this limit may be adjusted.

Then, you need to consider the credit utilization ratio. This is where your credit card balance is compared to your credit limit. Keeping the credit balance low can positively impact your credit score. Remember, the ratio should be below 30% for a healthy credit score.

To go back a few lines, the credit limit may increase. If your issuer notices that you have responsibly used your credit card, they may increase the limit. As much as this leads to bigger flexibility, it is also a bigger responsibility too - you still need to manage this correctly and avoid overspending.

Finally, the security of the credit card itself. As the chapter slowly comes to its end, we are going to see all the credit card security measures that are usually set in place. These are essential for preventing any unauthorized use of the credit card. As a credit card holder, you need to know its protection features - here they are:

- Monitoring for fraud - nowadays, there are sophisticated fraud detection systems that can monitor your activity and notice any fraudulent behavior. These systems are mostly flagging unusual behavior or transactions that are inconsistent with the regular behavior or transaction of the owner of the card (you).

- Zero liability protection - according to the federal law, the cardholders are usually not held liable for any unauthorized transactions made with their credit cards. Should this happen to you, you deem yourself protected simply by reporting it.

- EMV chip technology - EMV stands for Europay, Matercard, and Visa. Their chip technology has raised the bar on security features compared to the regular magnetic stripe cards. These chips hold a unique transaction code for each individual purchase. That makes it more difficult for any fraud to clone the card.

- Protected purchasing - all cards offer purchase protection benefits. These may vary - from price protection and coverage against theft or damaged items which are purchased with the card - it is all about understanding the limitations and terms so you can maximize their use.

However, even with these security measures in place, I would still advise you to monitor your credit card transactions and activities. The monthly statement, the account activity, and transaction alerts can help you react fast in case of an uncomfortable situation.

What did you learn from this chapter?

- The amazing power of credit cards
- What a credit score is and how to maintain a good one
- A part of delivering an accurate financial representation to yourself is frequently checking your credit reports.
- Interest rates - how they happen and how they affect you.

To conclude this chapter, the interest rates, the limits, the credit cards, and the credit scores are imperative for a responsible use of that little piece of plastic. To make an informed decision about it, you need to be familiarized with it first - which just happened!

However, after taking this chapter into account, it seems like one crucial topic has escaped us. After all, we talked about how to manage money, how to spend it wisely, and even how to save it and steer clear from financial trouble. But there's one thing we have yet to discover - how to make money. After all, you can't spend money if you don't have it in the first place, right? Turn the page to discover your best choices for becoming financially independent.

CHAPTER 6

HOW TO MAKE MONEY

"Money isn't everything, but it's right up there with oxygen."

— Zig Ziglar

As much as you hate to admit it, this is true – creating a comfortable lifestyle for yourself is not really an option if you don't have a steady and strong income. But, for some young adults, this is easier said than done. Even though we live in the era of technology, where everything is there, at the tips of your fingers, when it comes down to the actual part of making money, some of you may feel stuck. And I understand that. I was once where you are now – stranded in a sea of possibilities, yet still feeling like none of them suited me.

That changed when I started learning about how to make money. In the end, it turned out that it was an approach based on multiple viewpoints, one of them being the key point – determination. Instead of ignoring money and thinking that nothing will ever work for you, start focusing on prioritizing money and seeing how everything around you will start changing.

Let's delve into the chapter and learn all about how to make money and afford the lifestyle you want.

Cast a wide net - learn about all the ways you can generate income

The world of today is dynamic – it is filled with opportunities but also with an ever-changing job market. That leads to certain economic instabilities. The academic achievement you have made is excellent. Still, the process of obtaining a degree leaves you with a significant gap where you might have focused on honing the skills for the practical aspect of life, including generating income and financial literacy.

That is the reason why, when most students leave college, they are baffled with their choices and don't know where to proceed. They don't clearly understand how to leverage their skills and gain financial independence. This is the reason why it's important to focus on learning about finances, too. It is about you getting the wind beneath your wings to develop a unique and innovative approach that will expand your income-generating opportunities. That kind of mindset is what promotes growth and resilience whenever you are faced with a challenge.

First things first- take a look at the opportunities you have. As a young adult, you have more opportunities than you can imagine. However, most young adults walk the path that is the most familiar - which is also known as the broader concept of making money.

While you concentrate on finding the right job opportunity for you, you go through some of the most common (and popular) job options. These are all a good choice, and since you are at an early stage of your entrance into the workforce, you are in a very unique position. Here are the most common choices you can make in terms of choosing your income source.

- Getting a regular job - most young adults see getting a regular job as the perfect opportunity to reach financial independence. When it comes to picking a job, it can either be something you've learned to do your whole life or shifting your focus to monetizing a hobby of yours.

- Trying out freelancing - From an early age, you get to concentrate on finding various money vessels and even completely dismiss the concept of working the regular 9-5 job. Freelancing is the way to do that. With it, you have the unique opportunity to explore the various ways you can complete a job, without having to work the regular 40 hours a week. Freelancing can also help you cast an even wider net as you try communicating with people from all over the world and collaborate with them on various kinds of projects.

- Entrepreneurship - giving this one a go takes a lot of guts, but it might turn out to be one of the best ones for you. If you have a plan or an idea for a business (something that you can actively work on, at least in the beginning), entrepreneurship may be the right call for you. Acting on this idea may create the market disruption you need. It may also give you the opportunity to become visible to potential clients and competitors, thus developing a long-term vision for your financial life.

As you can notice, this book doesn't really delve deep into the regular jobs. The reason for that is because the regular job is just that - regular, something we are all familiar with. As a young adult, you most likely know how to get that kind of job already. I am here to help you cast a wider net, open your mind to new possibilities, and thrive. Now, let's move on to the main aspects you need to focus on to make the most out of your working journey.

<u>Think about your skills</u> - your skills are what separates you from the crowd. Define what you know and what you can offer as a product or a service, and then start from there. This is the most important aspect because it sets the groundwork for everything else you're going to do later on. Keep in mind, these can be more than one skill or passions. On most occasions, people mix a few of their passions to create something unique later on.

<u>Choose your niche</u> - as you can notice, these three aspects go hand in hand, as you can't move on from one to another. As you do these three in sync, you will realize that this third one is just as important. Choosing your niche means identifying exactly what you want to do based on your passions and skills. You have a particular expertise in a certain field, and don't be afraid to promote that.

<u>Network</u> - to spread the word about what you offer, to create a good web of people to work with, to dive deep into the freelance and entrepreneurship market, first you need to network. Do that by going to events where you can meet a lot of people who are more experienced in your field of choice. Talk to them, get their opinion, their experience, and avoid the mistakes they've been making.

Determining how you can make a grander effect in terms of freelancing and entrepreneurship takes a lot more than simply discovering what you know and love. After determining that, you can move on to the following:

1. Combine your skills and interests and come up with one or two things you can do, sell, or market online that would result in some income. This can be anything that you put your mind to – from graphic design to writing or maybe even teaching.

2. Explore the online platforms. This will help you choose the right platform where you can make the most out of your skillset and reach your desired audience. You can try platforms like YouTube, TikTok, or Etsy, depending on what you want to do.

3. Start working on developing your content. At the end of your brainstorming, there must be some product or service that you will be determined to offer. Create some content where you show your abilities, and make sure it is focused on the target group you want to attract. You can make blog posts, short videos, podcasts – anything you like.

4. Start building up your online presence. What does this mean? It means that if you want to generate a strong income, you need to focus on using social media channels to promote your content. Make your audience as engaged as possible and build your credibility one step at a time.

5. Finally, start to turn profits. The last step is selling your product or service, including ads in your blog, doing some affiliate marketing, offering some sponsored content, and reviewing products, etc.

This is the simple framework that can be used to build and promote almost any kind of venture you come up with.

Stepping away from the traditional 9-5 job and generating your income elsewhere takes time, determination, and thinking outside the box. However, this is still an option worth exploring because when you start, you seem to be given a blank canvas. You can do anything you want with it.

Delving deeper – side hustles

As a young mind that manages to shape their own future, so far you are doing great! You're stepping away from the familiarity that comes with having a regular job and you are creating something completely yours - from scratch. As you've established that, after some time, you might seem like you can take on some more work. Or you might even think that you still have other skills to show off, and to do this, you need to look into other job opportunities.

In the previous section, we only touched upon the subject of turning your interests into money-makers. The power of entrepreneurship and freelancing is great, and you can utilize it to the extent you need - as long as you determine the aspect you just read.

In this section, we will talk more about it – the power of the side hustle. It includes everything we mentioned earlier – from identifying your skills to monetizing them. You have probably noticed some of the more popular side-hustle options - product reviews, affiliate marketing, etc. The reason why the market has been seeing a lot of them lately is because of their high success rate – offering the perfect side hustle. If you decide to take this seriously, you will manage to sustain the lifestyle you want and never compromise on its quality.

First things first - what are side hustles? These are additional sources of income that people pursue along with their primary job. These are an excellent way to hone your skills, to try something new and exciting, and to create some new skills on top of the ones you've already acquired. But the thing is, even though many people are familiar with this concept, not many people turn to it - mostly because they don't know where to begin. Luckily for you, you have this book in your hands, so that shouldn't be an issue for you.

It's all about getting started easily. If you are still on the fence about it, here are a few things why you should do it, and a few tips to get you started.

- Yes, the additional income is always welcome, but there is also a potential opportunity for growth. By exploring various ideas, you also explore various potential ways of making money. It is the creative process that will spark up your imagination in unknown and wonderful directions.

- Tracking your finances while having extra security. For many people, developing a side hustle is both an enjoyment and a security blanket. You get to see how your ideas grow, and at the same time, the amount on your bank statement grows as well.

- Go after what you love. For some, it is more than just the money (though it is always a good addition). Sometimes, people get to explore themselves and discover a whole new range of things they want to do. Those things may not turn out to be full-time job material, so the side hustle is an excellent solution.

- It is a flexible endeavor. Stepping away into a non-traditional job terrain is the perfect choice for some people. Having a side hustle often comes with a flexible schedule and may allow you to do everything you want in a day.

- Creating an entrepreneurship future. As a concept, it allows you to bounce off of ideas without risking a lot. It can be the base upon which you may build a customer net and the chance to gain opportunities and even look to the future possibilities of launching your own business or businesses.

Generally, the side hustle can provide you with many benefits and open so many doors for you that you might end up creating a start-up from something you previously called a hobby. You get to enjoy some financial security, as this can be a way for you to develop a reasonable emergency fund or close off any debts you have. On top of everything, think about your own personal fulfillment! It is an unmatched feeling to know that you have started something from scratch and that you are working on it with every fiber of your being! It is a chance for both personal and professional development. You may not know exactly where you'll end up, but I promise you, if you are determined, it will be a good place.

Balancing multiple income streams and your personal life

It seems like there is a lot of talk about how to create the most out of your mind and hobbies and to use your free time to generate income. As a young adult, this might be more interesting to you than you can imagine. The thrill of finding out how you can create a solid income stream out of something you truly love is fascinating – and things get even better if you have more hobbies you can profit from. But when do you stop to say, "enough is enough"? Sometimes, and this happens especially among young people, plunging into the workforce and creating these new side hustles takes up so much of your time that you hardly ever have the time to turn around and check on yourself and your personal life.

When this happens, you may not realize it initially, but after a while, you may find yourself in the middle of a vortex you have difficulty getting out of. During your journey of creating a good professional future for yourself, it is important not to forget your personal life, too. Managing good relationships with yourself, your family, and your friends is the fuel that keeps you going in life, at least most of the time.

Creating solid streams of income, especially high income, requires constant and active involvement. Running a business is difficult and having a few of these sources to juggle may be a little too much to handle. In most professional experiences, managing a few side hustles at the same time can leave almost no time for maintaining a private life. That's when good organization comes into the picture.

There are three effective ways you can manage your multiple income streams and your private life – here they are.

1. Keep yourself organized

And I don't mean only a few days in the week – I mean all the time! Having an organized time means you can dedicate an exact amount of it to yourself, to work as you have planned, and to dedicate enough time to your family. Here, you can incorporate a few principles to make that happen, among which – you can start by setting realistic work goals. This is the easy bit, as many successful people do this. Your goals may be challenging, but they all need to be realistic. When you look at your tasks for the day, if you feel like someone else can do a better job at a few of those tasks, or you don't have the time to do all of them, it is more than okay to outsource them to other people, such as freelancers (as long as they are the right choice). That will help you maintain a better time management technique and work-life balance. Don't be scared of losing some of your profits. Freeing up your time is always a worthy investment, and most likely, the person you'll be working with will complete the tasks better than you would.

You should also know when you are working vs when you're not. No matter how much you try, you always seem to take the work home with you. You are working even when you're not supposed to – during dinner, during your quality time with yourself, and with the people you love. Having a workspace can help a lot, especially if you decide to run a few side hustles. You need to remember – when the time for work is over, it is really over.

That leads me to the next principle: having a separate space where you conduct your work. You can't work and relax from your own bed – you need to have a dedicated nook in the home (if you prefer working from home) and finish all your work there. This can help you disconnect when you need some time to relax and unwind. Without implementing this separation, you may end up struggling to find the balance between your work and your private life.

2. Take a step beyond being productive

What does this mean? It means always choosing efficiency over productivity. As you focus on setting up some incredible income streams for yourself, you may find yourself constantly making checklists and checking things off all the time. Doing this for a longer period may result in severe burnout. Instead of that, turn to a smarter approach – look at your goals rather than your journey, and brainstorm for some more efficient ways to achieve what you set out to do.

3. Define your motivation

Find out the reason why – why have you set out to achieve certain professional goals? Why do you take so much of your time to dedicate to it? Why do you want to create a work-life balance? The answers to these questions will lead you to define your motivation. They will lead you to work at full speed ahead but with a steady and determined mind.

Without clearly defining your motivation, you might have difficulty dedicating your hours. You may be working hard to provide for yourself or to help out your family – no matter what the cause, you need to have it clearly defined. That will crystalize the image for you, making it easier to dedicate just the right amount of time to work and for social connections.

What did you learn from this chapter?

- How to focus on money and prioritizing yourself.
- The importance of exploring various income-generating opportunities.
- The power of freelancing and entrepreneurship, and how to get started.
- How to make the most out of the best digital platforms today.
- Getting to know the power of the side hustle and how it can change your life and your mindset.
- How to refrain from giving it all in one place – creating the perfect balance between your professional and private life.

Making money may be a challenge for some of you, but as you can see from this chapter, it is all about finding the thing you want to do. You are a young adult, and you have both the time and the resources to explore until you discover the true you.

Once you do, all you need is to sit down, work and research a little bit, and set up the side hustle that may generate a lot of passive income. As soon as you know it, you might be looking into a decent amount in your bank account.

This is when the question may pose itself – what to do with all that money? Is there any way to expand your money-making ventures? If this question pops into your mind, then you're headed in the right direction! You're already thinking about the future, and I like that! In this book, the future is in the next chapter – because it is all about investing and multiplying the money you've made!

CHAPTER 7

HOW TO MULTIPLY YOUR MONEY – INVESTMENTS

"Personal finance is only 20% head knowledge. It's 80% behavior!"

— Dave Ramsey.

The uniqueness of approaching money comes from every individual's different perspective. But even in this case, we all have some things in common – starting from financial stability. Once you feel it, you want to make sure it lasts for as long as you live, right? So, you turn to various sources to figure out how to multiply your money and make it last as long as possible. In other words, you're investing in them.

This is a very positive money habit, right up there with creating a safety net and a budget. Investing is the peak reflection of your financial activities, and it is a combination of knowledge and behavior. Throughout this entire chapter you will be reading about investments - allow it to be the ultimate creative vessel through which your imagination will roam wild. While reading, you will learn about various ideas and ways you could get your money to grow.

That being the case, please don't take this as a definitive guide to investing. Why? Because this is a very deep and vast subject, and from this perspective, we are only talking about the tip of the iceberg here. To fully master investing you will need a lot more than this. If you want to apply yourself to this subject, you will need plenty of additional studying, and maybe even some assistance from a financial advisor.

While reading this chapter, you might discover you're already aligned with this on some points – that's your behavior. Learning about the rest – that's knowledge.

Let's dive in.

The basics of investing for beginners

Investing can be complex to understand, but it is the basis upon which personal finance is built. Learning this will help you keep track of the latest market movements and boost your confidence and your next financial moves.

The simplest way to explain this is to begin by understanding what you want and then just going for it. I reckon you need some more information at this time, so here is everything you need to do, explained in detail.

- You need to decide what your goals are – before you start looking into some investment options, you need to consider your overarching goals. Do you want to generate more income, or do you want to invest in something long-term? Once you decide on which option you want to take, it will narrow down your choices. This step of the process is about understanding your goals and the timeframe you need to achieve them. It will help you determine the risk you need to take and which aspect to prioritize. For example, if you want to invest in a retirement plan, then you need to take a look into your IRA and 401(k), whether your employer offers one, and how to get the most out of it.

- Choose your investment vehicles next – this can be one vehicle or more, depending on your goals. Think investing accounts. Think about developing a portfolio. Think brokerage accounts. With the help of the brokerage account, you can sell and buy stocks, ETFs, and mutual funds. This is a flexible way to invest, as there is no income limit or a limit on how much you can invest. There are also no rules if you want to withdraw your funds. The only drawback to it is that you do not have the same tax advantage as with retirement accounts.

  One thing to keep in mind here is that opening a brokerage account and only depositing money is not an investment. This is a common mistake a lot of young adults make, believing it is enough. But the final step here is to make a purchase.

- Determine the amount you want to invest – the goals you outline in the first step will help you determine how much you need to invest into each account. You should also check for investment limits depending on the accounts in question.

  Decide on the income percentage you want to invest. The general rule is to invest 15% of your yearly income toward your retirement goals, but depending on your income and your goals, this percentage can vary – as long as you invest a certain amount.

  Also, plan how you want to invest your money. A common question is: Do you want to invest all your money at once or equal amounts of money over time? The answer to this question will lead you to the right investment path.

- Measure your tolerance for risk. I am explaining this a little better below since it is an important step of the process.

It basically describes the level of risk you want to take as an investor for the potential of a higher return.

- I mentioned that you are an investor. Think about what kind of investor you want to be – when it comes to investing your money, there is not one approach that will fit everyone. It all depends on your goals, income, savings, knowledge, and willingness to take risks. With that in mind, you can either go for long-term or short-term investing.

    Short-term investing is trading, where you can opt for swing trading or day trading to make an instant profit. It is also the higher-risk option. Long-term investing will never really fall out of style since it gives you time to strategize, allows for a higher margin of error, and allows for more time for compounding interest.

- Develop a solid portfolio – the last step you're about to take in your investing process is to start combining your assets and see which assets will work the best to help you achieve your goals. Some of the most common investments you can add to your portfolio include bonds, mutual funds, stocks, and ETFs.

    As time passes, you want to monitor and rebalance your portfolio if necessary. Doing this allows you to relocate your funds to match your targeted allocation. Carefully follow the market so you won't go into a bad deal and lose money.

Understanding risk and return on investments

This is a trade-off that states how the potential of a bigger return increases when taking a bigger risk. By using this case, many people (not just young adults) associate low-risk levels with low returns and high-risk levels with higher potential returns. To understand this concept, you need to realize that the trading principle connects high risk with high reward. But, here, you should also understand that the people who turn to higher-risk steps have already come to terms with the fact that the investment may not work out.

However, there is some great potential in this, and to fully understand it, you also need to know that, even if some things don't work out with one investment, you can always go to the next one and make a better choice with that – the funds will return to you either way.

Some examples that include measuring singular risk in context include penny stocks and ETFs. For example, the penny stock may have a high risk on a singular basis, but if it only holds one spot in a wide portfolio, then the risk is minimal.

But the core where the risk-return trade-off exists is on a portfolio level. Once you create your portfolio, you will notice it combines risks and returns – some higher, some lower. Now, if you focus on the specific sectors by taking on single positions that represent a larger percentage of holdings, you can increase the risk and reward.

There are a few ways to calculate risk-return. Keep in mind that measuring risk-return investments is quite a complicated subject, and it is not the focus of this book. However, if you want to get started, make use of one of the following ratios below - these are very useful. You always have the possibility to expand your knowledge on that subject if you want to.

Alpha ratio – where you want to check the returns you've earned on an investment above the benchmark return. By using the alpha approach, you measure the excess returns.

Beta ratio – the beta ratio can show you how the stock's correlation stands against the benchmark that determines the overall market. This approach gives a lot of insight whenever you want to do some deeper analysis and check why a certain stock performs more or less in a certain period.

Sharpe ratio – this approach can help you determine if the risk you're taking is worth the reward you might be getting. It is used when you are comparing similar assets in your portfolio. This way, you take into account the degree of risk you might take (or have taken) and check whether it matches (or matched) your gains.

Different investment opportunities suitable for young adults

We're having all this talk about investments, portfolios, stocks, and all that when you are probably confused as they come, and you keep asking yourself one question – how to look for investing opportunities?

The sole idea of investing can be intimidating, especially if you are just starting. But, throughout your life, as you face new and challenging market environments, you look back to this moment and see how it was the perfect time to begin. We talked about risk assessment, so you don't need to jump into some wild rides in the very beginning. You can start as slow and as small as you want – of course, only until you get comfortable. While we are on that subject, let me help you explore some investment options that are suitable for you.

- High-yield savings account – this is probably the simplest way to boost your money return. You can open this account through an online bank, and all you need to know here is that these accounts tend to pay higher interest on average than the standard savings accounts. It is the perfect place to store your saved money and have them hold that for you for a few years, or until an emergency pops up.

- Certificate of deposit – this is another way for you to earn some additional interest on your savings, but in this case, be prepared to have your money tied up longer than you would with the high-yield savings account. If you opt for a certificate of deposit, then you will most likely not be able to touch your money before a certain time is up (this can vary anywhere from 6 months to 5 years or more) without having to pay a fine. That's why this approach is considered to be extremely safe.

- Retirement plan – this plan will benefit you in the future, it is probably one of the simplest ways to begin. You speak to your employer, you match a portion of what you agree to save from your regular paycheck, and that's it. These contributions are made before being taxed and they grow tax-free until you retire.

- Low-cost index funds and ETFs - these are perceived as one of the best beginner-friendly investments. These are designed to track a benchmark index and they don't require any professional expertise or knowledge. They function in a very interesting way - they don't try to beat the market, but rather flow with it and become the market. They are a low-risk investment that would result in a solid long-term return.

Remember the importance of compound interest

Let's continue to a section that can help you build your wealth over time. It is the concept of earning interest on both the interest and the principal amount. Sounds like something you never knew existed, right? Well, in this section, I will explain the basic concept of compound interest and how you can use it to maximize your savings.

Compound interest is a straightforward concept with which you can significantly change your savings. In the long run, it will result in significant growth. Take this as an example – you invest 1k USD at a 10% return, and you will earn 100 USD in interest in the first period. But, if you take that 100 USD and reinvest it, you will earn interest on both – so 10% of the 1k and 10% on the 100. Then, if you take the 110 USD you've made by reinvesting, you can expand the return base. In this case, it will be 10% on the 110, 10% on the 100, and 10% on the 1k. And so on – you can see the pattern here.

Need some help visualizing this in your mind? Here is a table that will make things a lot clearer for you.

Year	Principal	Interest earned	Total amount
1	$1000	$100	$1100
2	$1100	$110	$1210
3	$1210	$121	$1331
4	$1331	$133.1	$1464.1
5	$1464.1	$146.41	$1610.41
10	$2593.74	$259.37	$2853.11
20	$6727.50	$672.75	$7399.25
30	$17449.09	$1744.91	$19194

The compound effect is known by many because it can help you accumulate a significant amount of wealth with little to no effort from your end. Regular investing can help you grow your wealth in the long term.

There is a difference between simple and compound interest. Allow me to explain.

Simple interest is the interest you have earned on the principal amount only. It is mostly used for short-term loans or investments. Compound interest, on the other hand, is used for long-term investments, as you get an interest on your interest, too. It is critical to remain consistent here so you can build up your wealth – think 10, 20, 30 years from now.

So, which strategies can you implement to make this happen?

Start small and start as early as you can. As I mentioned, it is all about consistency because consistency is the principle of taking advantage of the compounding effect. Also, choose the right investment vessel. It is the thing that offers the best compound interest or return, such as stocks that pay dividends.

Constantly reinvest your money rather than taking it out – this way, you will allow for the investments to grow all the time. As previously mentioned, you can always invest in a retirement account, where your investments will grow tax-free until you retire. If you skip this for a few months, your end amount may be significantly lower than expected. Assuming that you miss doing this for a few months, you may lose hundreds of thousands in the end.

I recommend automating your savings and investment contributions. Nowadays, many banks allow this, making it a hassle-free activity that you don't ever have to think about.

Also, try to diversify your investments by utilizing various asset classes, such as real estate, bonds, and stocks, to maximize your long-term returns.

Last but not least – be patient. I know you are a beginner in this field but try not to make an impulsive investment decision based on some short-term fluctuations in the market. Use a compound interest calculator to see the potential impact that interest rates and strategies may have on your financial future.

Before we wrap up this chapter, let's examine another aspect – compound interest and debt. Is this a good combo, and how can you ensure you're on the right road? Compound interest is an excellent way to build wealth, but it can also be a tool that sets you back, especially if you have debt. Credit cards and loans use compound interest to calculate what you owe, and it can lead to a vicious cycle you can't get out of.

For example – you have a credit card with a 20% interest rate yearly and a 1k USD balance. You can only make the minimum payment. This situation will take you over 20 years to pay off the balance, and it will cost you more than 2k in interest charges. The compound interest here makes it more difficult to pay off the debt.

Understanding how compound interest works can help you achieve better financial freedom and independence, especially in the long run. It can also help you make the most of your finances in ways you could not have imagined.

What did you learn from this chapter?

- What is investing?
- The steps you need to take in order to start investing.
- Generally, the higher risk you take, the more it may pay off – and vice versa.
- The starter pack for investment – what are your safest options?
- Compound effect is your golden ticket for long-term wealth growth.

Investing your money, no matter how unknown a terrain may be, is always an exciting one. You get the unique opportunity to learn all about yourself through your portfolio. You learn how to manage and tweak it by keeping a close eye on the market, as well as learning how and when to take risks (that will hopefully pay off in unimaginably good ways). However, it is time to move to some uncharted territory – yet again.

We have come to the part of the book that most people dread. The following chapter is a very important one, so you must not skim through it. It is about taxes – something that every person needs to know about (and pay). Turn the page, and let's go through them together.

CHAPTER 8

THE ONE THING WE ALL HAVE IN COMMON – TAXES

"In this world, nothing can be said to be certain, except death and taxes."

— Benjamin Franklin

You are probably familiar with this saying – whether you've heard it from your parents, guardians, teachers, relatives, or a stranger – everybody knows that taxes must be paid.

This may seem a little strange. Instead of congratulating you on your first job, we are here talking about some of its most important aspects (that don't include the actual work). You should pay your taxes no matter what your work or where you live – that means yes, you still need to pay taxes even if you still live with your parents.

Before we begin, here are a few things you need to know:

- Everyone pays taxes all over the world. In the USA, you are required to pay taxes on all income, no matter the source.

That means that you should even submit for income taxes even if you have done some yard work or babysitting.

- The income tax is paid via deduction from your paycheck as you earn it.

- It helps to keep an expense record, as it can help you file an exact annual tax return with the IRS* (this is only in America) before the 15th of April every year. This tax return is based on your income and expenses.

What is the IRS? - IRS is an abbreviation from the Internal Revenue Service. It is an agency based in the U.S. that applies federal tax laws and collects federal taxes from both individuals and companies all across the country. All U.S. citizens are taxpayers, and the tax is paid on an annual level.

Already sounds complicated, doesn't it? Don't worry about it. There is a high probability that your first few tax returns will be very simple, taking into consideration your financial situation. As a young person, you are more likely to have one source of income, and even in this case, there are plenty of ways to minimize the tax you owe.

In this chapter, you will learn all about the implications and how to start early and work early on your taxes. By the end, you will realize that it is easy.

Basics of taxation and their implications on personal finances

Since we are starting from square one, let's answer one question: what are taxes?

Taxes are what you call a "mandatory contribution" to the government entity – this can be local, regional, or national government. We pay taxes because the tax revenues are (most of the time) the primary and sole contributor to any kind of public work – from government activities to building roads and schools and programs such as Medicare.

In the economic world, taxes are the burden that befalls the person who is responsible for them – this can be a person or a business. If we look at this from an accounting perspective, there is a vast array of taxes to consider, some of which include state income taxes, sales taxes, payroll taxes, federal taxes, etc.

Below, you can find some of the most common types of taxes. Learn them, because you should know them!

- Income taxes – giving a percentage of the income you've generated to your state or federal government.

- Payroll taxes – the percentage from the paycheck that the employer withholds from the employee, which is paid to the government on the employee's behalf to fund healthcare and social security programs.

- Corporate taxes – the percentages taken from corporate profits by the government to fund any federal programs.

- Sales taxes – these vary by jurisdiction, but they are levied on specific goods and services.

- Property taxes – depend on the value of the property and the land you own.

- Estate taxes – this is something that applies whenever the property of a person who just died needs to be evaluated, and the total estate has to exceed thresholds that are set by federal and state governments.

- Tariff – also known as taxes on imported goods (added with the belief that it can strengthen domestic business).

The tax system varies greatly from nation to nation, but all of them follow the same rule – everyone needs to pay it. So, before you become a part of the workforce and eligible to pay taxes, you need to study them carefully and know what they're all about. Depending on your current situation, you might even need to pay various taxes.

If we take the USA as an example, how do taxes work exactly? Well, first things first, US taxes are generally known to be lower than in other nations. Only a few years ago, the US tax revenue represented 24% of the Gross Domestic Product (GDP), according to official information, in contrast to other countries, where the average percentage was 34%. In the USA, the taxation increases progressively as your income grows. The tax brackets currently range between 10 and 37 percent, depending on your income.

Okay, now that we have the taxes out of our way, let's talk about taxation. The act of taxation is a term that explains the government imposing a financial obligation on its residents and citizens. You are already aware that people have been paying taxes for a long time now. What the term taxation means is that it applies to all types of mandatory levels, from income taxes to estate taxes.

When you look at it independently, taxation varies from other forms of payment (for example, market exchange) because it is directly connected to any service rendered and does not require consent. However, taxation is not extortion or racket because the imposing institution is the government, not a private entity. Taxation and the formulation of tax policies nowadays are considered to be one of the most critical aspects of modern politics.

History time – taxes in the USA

The American government was originally funded on a very small amount of direct taxation. Instead of that, the federal agencies turned to user fees for government properties. But, when times started getting tough, the government would sell bonds and assets or issue an assessment of the taxes for the rendered services.

The justification for taxation has always been the same. Since the early taxes began, they have been used to raise armies, build defenses, rule classes, and so on. However, as society progressed forward, the justification expanded to economic, utilitarian, and moral considerations. Nowadays, some products and services (for example, gasoline and tobacco) have a higher tax than others. People who have advocated for taxes on public goods theorize that this financial imposition is necessary in case the private provision of public goods is considered to be less than optimal.

At this point in the chapter, you know what taxes are; you know why everyone pays them, but you are still not sure why you're paying them. Here, we go back to the first sentence of this chapter – Benjamin Franklin's words of wisdom. Taxation has been considered the bedrock of modern society since the dawn of time. To live in a society as advanced as the one we have today, we are all paying taxes. You will start paying your taxes so you can enjoy driving the roads, using healthcare, using the public schools, and knowing there is an entire force set in place to protect you (should things ever go wrong). While we, as a society, help the governments fund various undertakings, we can go to bed calmly, knowing that we've done our part in the process of advancing as a whole.

Tax-filing process and common deductions for young adults

We've come to the section where you need to learn how to actually do your taxes. From what you've seen so far from the people around you, it is a hectic process, but once we go through it together, you will realize how simple it is.

Tax filing is something people do every year, and instead of leaving it all to chance and guessing, now we're going to learn how to fill out the annual tax returns.

The tax obligations vary from one individual to the next. Some people may receive a refund on taxes. Others may owe money. That is why you need to know how to complete your taxes correctly from the start and save yourself a headache. Before beginning, you need to check which forms you need with the IRS and verify the deadlines for filing.

The main points you need to explore are:

- Filing status
- Paperwork
- Method

Let's begin.

Filing status – choosing this can help you determine the amount of money you owe, and the different statuses have various tax brackets. If more than one status applies to you, one of them may reduce your tax obligations more than the other one. IRS mainly divides the individuals into the following groups:

- Single – these are all the unmarried taxpayers, including the ones that are legally separated and divorced. The single-filer status also applies to those individuals who do not meet the requirements for head of household status.
- Married filing together – joint filing status means that you are filing the taxes for both incomes combined – your spouse's and yours.

- Married filing individually – those who do not qualify for the joint married filing file their taxes separately. This happens in those cases where spouses prefer to keep their finances separate.

- Head of household – as you can imagine, you can apply for a head of household status if you are single and unmarried with at least one qualifying dependent (a child, a relative such as an older parent, or a sibling with a disability).

- Qualified widow(er) – anyone whose spouse passed away in the year before the current tax year. This taxpayer should also have a child or a stepchild (dependent).

Paperwork – when you're doing your taxes, you need to know how to file all the tax return paperwork correctly. By that, I mean gathering the necessary information and filling it out correctly. Filing taxes correctly means filing a lot of paperwork. You usually receive tax forms for the previous year from your employer, lenders, clients, and financial institutions from January of the current year. There is usually a deadline to file your taxes; in most cases, that deadline is in April. I took the USA as an example here, as this applies there. However, even if I am dissecting the US tax return as an example, that doesn't mean you don't pay taxes if you are in another country - on the contrary. Take a look below at all the forms US citizens use to file their taxes, and which ones are used in which particular cases.

- Income – you need to report your income from every source (remember, this can either be one or multiple sources) using some of the most common income reporting forms. They are:

  - **Form 1040** – This is used to complete your individual tax return.

- **Form W-2** – This is used to fill out the Wage and Tax Statement – everything made as an employee from an employer, and it also includes taxes withheld, including state, medical, federal, and Social Security taxes.

- **Form 1099-NEC and 1099-MISC** – Under this category are all non-employee and miscellaneous compensation – from attorneys to freelancers, landlords, and contractors.

- **Form 1099-INT** – This includes taxes on investment expenses, tax-exempt interest, interest income, withdrawal penalties, and other amounts associated with interest earnings.

- **Form 1099-DIV** – This records taxes for dividends and distributions.

- Deductions – these can lower your taxable income. You either get a standardized deduction or an itemized deduction. The standardized deduction varies depending on your filing status and the amount you have filed. You can check that to see if you are eligible for a standard deduction. On the other hand, the itemized deduction can be anything where you save receipts and documentation for transactions you want to deduct – such as mortgage interests, extra medical expenses, charitable donations, etc.

- Credits – the deductions may lower your taxable income. Still, the credits can directly reduce your entire tax bill and, with that, completely lower your tax liability (even more than you ever could with a deduction). In the US, some popular tax credits can do this for you:
  - Child and dependent care tax credit
  - Earned income tax credit
  - Premium tax credit
  - American Opportunity Tax credit

<u>Method</u> – mainly, there are three ways for you to file your taxes – the method you choose is based on your tax situation and how comfortable you are with filing your taxes.

1. IRS – (again, this is the specific case of the USA) you can file your taxes using Form-1040 with the IRS. Through some partnered websites, you can even file your taxes electronically. There is a step-by-step guide on filing your taxes there, but the fileable forms still require a deeper knowledge of filing taxes. In some countries, the tax officials offer an online platform where you can fill out your tax forms.

2. Software – if you need some help to file your taxes, remember that you don't have to do it alone. Some software programs are incredibly popular nowadays, and they can help you get the correct tax deductions and credits based on your current situation.

3. Tax Professional – knowing how to do taxes is an incredibly valuable skill. If you want to do this right, you can always turn to a professional to help you. That way, you know you can complete your tax return correctly. You don't have to have an account for the entire year; you can only hire an accountant for that particular occasion.

As a young adult, this next bit is exactly what you need – the most common tax deductions. It's important to know what you can deduct as a young adult, so here is the list that will get you started. Here are some of the most common tax deductions:

1. If the employer does not reimburse them – moving expenses.

2. Self-employment tax (as a part of a self-employment taxpayer).

3. Retirement plan contributions as a self-employed individual.

4. Real estate tax.

5. Contributions to charity.

6. Expenses for having an office at home.

7. Tax on any type of vehicle.

8. State and local income taxes.

9. Unreimbursed employee expenses.

10. Student loan interest.

11. Fees and tuition (if you are not claiming an education credit).

12. If you are a homeowner, mortgage interest.

There is also something called tax credits for young adults. In this case, you need to remember that not all tax benefits can qualify as deductions. As a young adult, you can qualify for some tax credits. These include the credits that I mentioned above. Depending on your unique situation, you can check which ones you are eligible for.

There are some things you cannot deduct. No matter how much you try, some things are simply not deductible. These are, for example, personal expenses. So, everything you can think of, such as – clothes, personal grooming, health club, gym membership, groceries, fines, penalties, event tickets, home furnishings – are not deductible. Thankfully, some expenses can still be tax-deducted if you know where to look. Depending on the circumstances, you can dig a little deeper and find these situations. You need to know exactly what you are looking for since this is not always clear-cut. You can get some help from a professional or anyone who has a deeper understanding of the tax law to lend you a hand. Here are a few examples of the exceptions:

- Cell phone – you can get a deduction on your new smartphone. It is not deductible if you get it for your personal use, but it may be deductible if you use it for work or business. It all depends on the facts and circumstances. If you are a self-employed taxpayer and want to get a phone to use for business, then you can deduct the phone. But, if you are an employee and not a business owner, the deduction can only go to the extent that the total exceeds 2% of the taxpayer's gross income.

- Costs for a start-up – you can deduct a few thousand dollars if you are a small business owner.

- Professional expenses and continuing education – naturally, almost all that should be reimbursed by the employer, but if it is not, it can be deducted. But, for example, bar examination fees are not deductible.

- Expenses with a side job – since there are a million ways to enjoy the benefits of a side hustle nowadays, people turn to it the most because any expense that is ordinary and necessary to conduct that business can be deducted. As a taxpayer, remember that information to support your tax file.

- Medical expenses for the elderly – when you pay medical expenses for an elderly parent, you are eligible for a deduction the same way your parents would be eligible for a deduction if you were in each other's place.

- Deduction on clothes – there is still a way you can be eligible for a clothing deduction – if it is required as a condition of employment, and it cannot be adapted for general use as ordinary clothing. The best example is in the case of required uniforms.

Noticing even the smallest details and doing your due diligence can help you reach your goal and claim a deduction on your taxes. Everything you do has its own set of requirements, and some of them can be complex, so always be careful and mindful of the details.

Tips and strategies for minimizing tax liability

Tax liability is the debt or amount of money you owe to the government in taxes as an individual or anyone else. Generally, the term "tax liability" is mostly used to refer to federal income tax liability. In other words, if your income is very low, you won't have any tax liability whatsoever.

How does this apply to you as a young adult?

You can minimize your tax liability by taking a few steps. In this section, I am serving you the best tips and strategies to do that and get the most out of your tax experience. Here's what you can do:

1. Increase your contributions to your retirement – the income tax you pay every year is based on the gross income you have. Gross income is the total amount of money before any credits, taxes, or deductions are accounted for. If you want to reduce this number, then the best thing you can do is contribute to the employer-sponsored retirement plan or the traditional individual retirement plan – also known as IRA. Suppose the employer plan is not available to you. In that case, you can make contributions with the pre-taxed money, which will directly reduce your taxable income and contribute to your total tax liability in the end.

2. Investment losses turned into profits – this seems a little illogical, but it can be done. If you have some investments that have declined in value since you purchased them, you can sell them – that will reduce your tax liability for

the year. This is a very well-known strategy, also known as tax-loss harvesting. In the end, these investment losses will be written off against your investment gains or any other income up to a certain limit every year. Any losses that you cannot take advantage of in the current year – you can carry into your future years and reduce your taxes then.

3. Donating – charities are a great way to reduce your taxes, but only if you itemize deductions on your tax returns and don't go the route of standard deduction. The contribution you make to a qualified charitable organization can be anything from used household items, to goods, or to cash, but keep in mind – any donation that has a value over $250 needs a receipt.

Your tax liability is your tax bill. It may seem like you owe a lot to the government at the beginning, but you can take plenty of steps to minimize that amount. These three steps are the most commonly used ones and the ones you may benefit from the most.

What did you learn from this chapter?

- What are taxes, why everyone needs to pay them, and why are you paying them?
- What taxation means, and why is it used?
- A detailed guide on how to do your taxes.
- The most common deductions for young adults.
- Paying attention to details matters, especially in the case of filing your taxes.
- Not everything can be tax-deducted.
- What is tax liability and how to successfully minimize your tax liability.

There's a very high chance that you have to pay taxes, especially if you have a steady source of income. Any money you've earned from an employer will result in a tax bill. Of course, nobody wants to pay the government more than they should, so this is where learning about taxes comes into the picture.

But as people say, "The storm is behind us," You may not realize it now, but learning all there is to know about taxes will result in you setting sail in the deep financial waters with experience, knowledge, and ease.

It is all about making you feel more confident with money – talking about them, handling them, keeping them, and letting go of them when necessary. The following chapter is one you will hold dear for the rest of your life – as we reach high until we grab your financial independence!

CHAPTER 9

REACH YOUR FINANCIAL INDEPENDENCE

"Money, like emotions, is something you must control to keep your life on the right track."

— Natasha Munson.

A t the end of the day, financial freedom is something a lot of people dream about. However, actually executing it and becoming financially stable as a young adult takes a lot of courage, knowledge, and persistence. The careful guide you need to create for yourself requires a lot of focus and attention to detail – and that's exactly what we will do in this chapter.

In this final one, I will help you create the best strategies for achieving financial independence as a young adult.

Achieving financial independence at a young age

Being a financially secure person for the rest of your life and achieving that at a young age may sound like a stretch. But, it is not an uncommon practice – a lot of people have done it – the thing is, they don't kiss and tell. So naturally, when you are a young adult struggling to reach financial knowledge and independence, you often feel stuck in a loop you can't get out of. That's understandable because, at the point you're at, you may not have the necessary skills or knowledge to achieve what you want.

That doesn't mean you shouldn't work for it. This book is filled with all kinds of information that will help you become a master of your finances, and these final strategies are the icing on the cake you never knew you needed.

This concept is filled with some remarkably strong strategies that can help you achieve financial security before you even turn 30! No worries. Even if you're a little late to the party, you can still join in!

1. Track how much you spend – the only thing that will keep your spending in check is effectively tracking how much you spend. If you don't want to reach for that pen and paper and write things down – we live in the age of technology! Open your phone and search for any free budgeting app so you can get started.

    Writing down how much you spend is something that can prevent you from wasting the money you've worked so hard to earn. For example, once you see your total bill for all the days you've ordered food instead of making a meal at home, you might rethink deleting that delivery app from your phone.

2. Living within your boundaries – everybody wants something. Everybody wants everything. But of course, not everybody can get everything they want – and for now, neither can you. Take a moment to look through your living standards. Are you spending more than you

earn? Do you allow yourself some expensive goods and services? Can you really afford them, or are you piling up the expenses on multiple credit cards? We've discussed the credit card situation, and now you know it is a bad debt you should get out of as soon as possible. If you want to gain financial independence, you should manage your expectations. Start by reducing your debt and adding more to your savings account. It will do wonders for you both long-term and short-term.

3. Avoid borrowing money – yes, you do have a certain set of standards and a certain lifestyle to maintain, but there is nothing worse than lending money to make it happen. Financial independence doesn't come from borrowing more than you can return. If you want to continue that practice, at least make something of it – invest in yourself. For example, you can invest in your education and your business to get a piece of real estate, etc. In these cases, if you borrow money, it can help you get the leverage you need to reach your financial goals faster than usual. So, it's not about creating a lifestyle you cannot afford, but rather creating something out of it.

4. Short-term goals – one of the best strategies you can implement while you turn your financial life into magic is this one. There are more than just a handful of things that can happen to you as a young adult. Life can throw many curveballs your way, and you won't be able to catch them all. This is when the long-term planning concept comes into the picture. But what about the short-term goals? You can have those set into place, too.

The best way to start is with a series of short-term goals that are measurable, achievable, and precise. You don't have to do something big – paying off a small debt is the perfect starting point – or saving a certain amount of money in your account. Once you see you can easily do that, you will have a larger chance of achieving your long-term goals. Write down the list of goals and start working toward achieving them!

5. Be financially literate – to make money is sometimes easy – but to know what to do with them can be a challenge for most of you. Thankfully, through all our planning in the previous pages, now you know the area of personal finances that will pay off for the rest of your life. Knowing how to make solid financial and investment decisions is an important strategy that can help you achieve all your financial goals.

6. Save for retirement – since I already mentioned this a few times throughout the book, I cannot stress how important it is. I know that planning for your retirement may be the last thing on your mind at the moment, but if you only take a few steps to make it happen, it will work for you right up to the moment when you blow out the candles on your "Happy Retirement" cake. Even if you decide to save a small amount of money, if you do this early in your life, it will make a difference later on. The contribution plans you make and what we discussed earlier (compound interest) will help you set up a pretty good sum of money for retirement.

7. Don't be afraid to take risks – as long as they are calculated. When you are young, a lot of things can happen – you may get the opportunity to move to a new place, invest in some high-return stocks, take jobs at various companies, and so on. Some things will be a mistake, but some won't. To be on the safer side, you need to take some calculated risks. That way, even if you

do make a mistake, you have a lot of time to recover from it. A calculated risk is going back to school for additional training and accepting that job offer that pays more (even though it is in a different city).

8. Keep investing in your biggest asset – you – the thing is, many people turn to the things they want to achieve without looking at themselves first. It is all about paving the way for yourself to move forward, and this can be anything in terms of upgrading your skill set, your knowledge, and your experience. This is a bullet-proof strategy – meaning you will continually upgrade your value in the job market and will keep making smart choices.

This is a sort of investment that begins in college, and after you've finished it, you should keep upgrading your skills and make sure they are up to date with what the job market needs. It is a lifelong practice but will keep you on the higher-paying end of the workforce.

9. Balance things out – at the end of the day, you are still a young adult – but that doesn't mean you should stop enjoying yourself altogether and focus only on financial stability. It is all about finding the perfect balance between what you spend today and how much you invest for the future. As the last strategy on the list of gaining financial independence early in life, consider it a constant reminder that you should, after all – live. The short-term goals, along with all the other strategies, make up for the perfect plan you can start working on.

The FIRE concept

Understanding the concept of Financial Independence Retire Early, or for short, FIRE, is a movement that revolves around the idea that anyone can achieve financial freedom at a young age. However, this movement takes it to a little bit of an extreme level, where you are supposed to live below your means, save a larger portion of your finances, and invest the saved money into something that will generate a passive income for years to come.

If you want to become a follower of the FIRE plan, then you may be able to retire much earlier than anticipated. However, this approach includes saving up to 70% of your monthly income to your account while still being a full-time part of the workforce. You continue doing that (by living your day-to-day life on the bare minimum) until your savings reach approximately 30 times what you spend in a year (that makes about a million dollars for an average salary). That means you can retire early or quit any form of job employment.

There are more variations to this approach, but the one thing people seem to try out the most is cutting back on their expenses as much as possible. Instead of spending, they put their money aside to invest them – ultimately making the best choice ever. They continue to be an active part of the workforce, but the only alteration they make is – they don't retire that early.

Long-term financial planning and retirement

Have you heard of the term "Failing to plan is planning to fail?" This rings out to be particularly true, especially in the case when you don't make some long-term financial planning or retirement plans. The economic landscape we live in today is quite a complex one. And that is why it is crucial to adopt a more proactive approach. You need to know how to manage your personal finances to the point where you will secure yourself a retirement. In this segment, you are going to learn how to underline the significance of long-term financial planning and retirement, accentuate the risks connected to it, and successfully avoid them.

Let's separate the two so we can focus on one thing at a time.

Long-term financial planning

Let's be honest from the beginning – you are already familiar with what you need to do here, but let's go over the points one more time.

- You need to set a goal – whether it is a short-term or long-term goal, as long as you have it, it can help you create a map that will lead to your financial independence. The goal can be anything you want, from planning a retirement fund to buying a home. It should be a clear and have concise goals that give you the motivation to work for it.

- Manage your cash flow – the cash flow represents everything – your income, savings, expenses, as well as miscellaneous occurrences. Keeping track of it (budgeting it) can help you prevent any overspending and can nudge you in the right direction of the long-term plans you have.

- Manage your debt, too – in fact, make it a priority. If you don't manage your debt properly, then you might hinder your financial progress and jeopardize your long-term plans. Make a repayment plan, prioritize it, and keep as far away as possible from going into more debt.

- Insurance, risk management, the works – this is a vital component of long-term financial planning. It involves assessing any potential risks and adding some insurance coverage so you can mitigate them. Think life insurance, health insurance, disability insurance, and property insurance. These are staples if you want to protect yourself from any unforeseen events that may put a dent in your financial plan.

Retirement planning

There is a specific significance to learning how to make the most out of your retirement plan. Yes, I believe everyone should have one, and instead of worrying about it, all you need to know are a few aspects, most of which we have mentioned before.

- Consider the changing economic landscape – as life expectancy increases, retirement planning has become a very popular choice for a lot of people. Since you might enjoy a longer retirement period, you might want to carefully plan your finances to achieve that.

- Social security considerations – the benefits you may get from your employer can provide you with some financial support in your retirement, but this is often not enough to meet all your expenses. When planning early retirement, you can fill the gap between the retirement income you expect and the lifestyle you desire by adding a lot of additional savings through your retirement accounts and investment vehicles.

    These investment vehicles can be anything from 401(k) plans, other employer-sponsored plans, IRAs (Individual Retirement Accounts), stocks, bonds, mutual funds, and more.

- Consider the ever-changing inflation and healthcare costs – while you save for retirement, keep in mind that you need to factor in the rising healthcare costs and inflation. Retirement is a long-term investment, emphasizing the importance of long-term insurance when you are gradually developing a retirement fund can potentially protect your savings.

Retirements plans in the U.S.

I previously mentioned 401(k) plans and IRAs. Before we conclude this chapter, let's talk about them a little more. Do you know what they are and how can you utilize them? Here is a brief explanation for both of them.

401(k) is also known as an employer-sponsored retirement plan. Employers usually offer the 401(k) and it tends to match the contribution of the employee. The contributions are made before taxes, which means that the total amount of the contributions reduces after being taxed.

With the IRAs, things are different. IRA is an abbreviation for an individual retirement account. If you want to open one, you can do that through a brokerage firm or a bank. Here, you don't have any kind of contribution from an employer.

One thing to keep in mind - you can invest both the 401(k) and the IRA in stocks, securities, and bonds.

So, as you can see, there are many ways you can plan for the future. Your primary plan should always be - investing in yourself and trying to be financially independent and free from a young age. After that, after you've felt like you are standing on solid ground, you can look further into the future - as far as the retirement plans.

What did you learn from this chapter?

- That financial independence at a young age is possible with a lot of planning and determination.

- Some of the best strategies that can help you achieve financial independence.

- What FIRE stands for – a new concept that a lot of people adopt.

- How to focus on long-term financial planning and retirement.
- What is a 401(k) and IRAs?

At the beginning of this chapter, achieving financial freedom and independence as an early adult may have seemed like a very ambitious goal. But after all the possibilities and strategies you discovered here, you can see that it is not impossible to achieve. Everything you want is always within reach. By understanding what you need to do – from setting clear financial goals to investing smartly, exploring multiple income sources, and planning your retirement – you can take the steering wheel and fully control your financial future.

Even if you make some mistakes along the way, holding your balance while you try to achieve your goal is key – and knowing you have the tools and resources to do that just makes things better!

CONCLUSION

"You either master money or, on some level, money masters you."

— Tony Robbins

How do you feel now? Do you feel ready to have it all? Let's briefly review everything you've learned from this book.

The first thing you did was – you learned how to get into the right mindset. Also, you learned there is a specific mindset to get into in the first place. Financial success requires a lot of determination and perseverance, as well as developing a solid perspective. Without it, you will not know which direction to take next. Once you discovered you had some goals, and you brought them onto the surface and wrote them down, you started learning about the compound effect, too. As a concept, this was an eye-opener for you – broadening your horizons to an extent you never knew could be possible.

Then, you realized that your journey would be filled with ups and downs, for you reached the second milestone and immediately started focusing on "what if – the negative version." It is important to know you have the ability to prepare for rainy days, and it costs more to let go of everything and simply go with the flow. You realize you do not want that. The opposite of that kind of behavior is planning, understanding, and managing financial tasks and risks.

With that in mind, the only logical next step was to start setting clear and achievable financial goals – and you managed to execute that beautifully and with ease. The basics of budgeting seem like a piece of cake to you now – what you thought would be quite difficult to overcome was to set and stick to a budget. But, with a few meticulously planned strategies, you discovered there is an easy way to do that, too!

Naturally, before you step into the workforce yourself and exhibit the powerhouse that you are, you learn about debt. This is often a phrase that not a lot of people want to use, talk about, or even think about. But talking and thinking about debt means you have a deeper understanding of the finance subject as a whole. A young adult such as yourself should not be scared by debt but should have the power to differentiate between the good and the bad – which you mastered instantly.

Finally, you reached the point that you were waiting for so long – the book's core and why you picked it up in the first place – how to make money. You have to learn all there is to know about main hustles, side hustles, various job opportunities, and what you need to look for in your unique situation. When exploring multiple income-generating opportunities, you realize what I mentioned in the beginning – this journey will be filled with ups and downs. Balancing multiple income streams with your personal life is as important as the action of making money itself. Now you know how to avoid being in that position where you will only focus on your jobs and nothing else.

Once you start to make money, the only logical next step is to learn how to manage it properly, right? So, I dedicated an entire chapter to investing and laid out a solid plan that could help you multiply your money. As you can see from the chapter, it wasn't anything complicated or difficult. All it took was a little bit of explaining and a few good examples, and you easily got the hang of it.

When you take an active part in the workforce, you must pay taxes. You probably already knew this even before you started reading this book. People talk about taxes all the time – and for a good reason. It is the one thing you absolutely have to do, and the one thing that will stick with you for the rest of your life. Rather than it being a choice, it is an obligation – and the sooner you understand that the better the financial future you will have.

Last but not least, you reached the final chapter of this book, and you learned how to reach financial independence as well! From short-term planning to long-term planning, I managed to cover all the important aspects of finances and gave you the perfect strategies that can help you reach financial independence while you're still a young adult.

Now, with all your newfound knowledge, there is no wonder you have more confidence and are able to approach finances with a smile on your face – you know what you're doing now! It feels like you've inhaled a breath of fresh air, doesn't it? Learning all you've read here usually takes up a lot of time, effort, and energy. But you managed to crash course finances and become literate in a short period of time. I hope that, from this day on, you will take this book as the pillar of your financial knowledge, and you will only upgrade yourself with experience from here on. Finally, you can't wait to get on your financial journey because you already feel like a winner.

One last thing. I still haven't received an answer from you. Are you ready to have it all now?

THANK YOU

Thank you so much for purchasing my book.

The marketplace is filled with dozens and dozens of other similar books but you took a chance and chose this one. And I hope it was well worth it.

So again, THANK YOU for getting this book and for making it all the way to the end.

Before you go, I wanted to ask you for one small favor.

Could you please consider posting a review for my book on the platform? Posting a review is the best and easiest way to support the work of independent authors like me.

Your feedback will help me to keep writing the kind of books that will help you get the results you want. It would mean a lot to me to hear from you.

Leave a Review on Amazon US →

Leave a Review on Amazon UK→

ABOUT THE AUTHOR

Emily Carter is an author who loves helping teens with their biggest turning point in life, adulting. She grew up in New York and is happily married to her high school sweetheart. She also has two of her own children.

In her free time, Emily is an avid volunteer at a local food bank and enjoys hiking, traveling, and reading books on personal development. With over a decade of experience in the education and parenting field she has seen the difference that good parenting and the right tips can make in a teenager's life. She is now an aspiring writer through which she shares her insights and advice on raising happy, healthy, and resilient children, teens, and young adults.

Emily's own struggles with navigating adulthood and overcoming obstacles inspired her to write. She noticed a gap in education regarding teaching essential life skills to teens and young adults. She decided to write comprehensive guides covering everything from money and time management to job searching and communication skills. Emily hopes her book will empower teens and young adults to live their best lives and reach their full potential.

To find more of her books, visit her Amazon Author page at:

https://www.amazon.com/author/emily-carter

REFERENCES

Money Skills for Teens

Allinson, M. (2023, January 18). *Why is money important in our lives? Robotics & Automation* News. https://roboticsandautomationnews. com/2023/01/18/why-is-money-important-in-our-lives/59144/

Bank of America. (2019). *Creating a budget with a personal budget spreadsheet. Better Money Habits.* https://bettermoneyhabits. bankofamerica.com/en/saving-budgeting/creating-a-budget

Bell, A. (2022, April 7). *What are the 5 purposes of budgeting?* Investopedia. https://www.investopedia.com/financial-edge/1109/6-reasons-why-you-need-a-budget.aspx#:~:text=Having%20a%20budget%20 keeps%20your

Blinka, D. (2023, February 2). *How to calculate and compare unit prices at the store.* WikiHow. https://www.wikihow.com/Calculate-and-Compare-Unit-Prices-at-the-Store

Bowling, L. (2019, February 22). *How much should i spend on clothing?* Financial Best Life. https://financialbestlife.com/how-much-should-i-spend-on-clothing/

Braverman, B. (2022, May 10). *Big purchases need major planning. here's where to start | CNN business.* CNN. https://edition.cnn. com/2022/05/10/success/save-for-a-big-purchase/index.html

Drury, P. (2022, January 25). *25+ jobs for teens (with job search advice).* Resume.io. https://resume.io/blog/jobs-for-teens

FarmWell. (n.d.). Financial wellbeing: *Developing a healthy money mindset.* FarmWell. https://farmwell.org.uk/wp-content/uploads/ sites/2/2022/03/Financial-Wellbeing-Developing-a-Healthy-Money-Mindset.pdf

Fernando, J. (2023, March 9). *Bond: Financial meaning with examples and how they are priced.* Investopedia. https://www.investopedia.com/ terms/b/bond.asp

Frankenfield, J. (2019). *Online banking*. Investopedia. https://www.investopedia.com/terms/o/onlinebanking.asp

Ganatra, M. (2022, September 27). *How to analyze your options before buying an insurance policy*. Forbes Advisor INDIA. https://www.forbes.com/advisor/in/life-insurance/how-to-analyze-your-options-before-buying-an-insurance-policy/

Gongala, S. (2014, July 25). *21 essential life skills for teens to learn*. MomJunction; MomJunction. https://www.momjunction.com/articles/everyday-life-skills-your-teen-should-learn_0081859/

HappyBank. (n.d.). *Financial tips: Six steps to creating a positive money mindset*. Happy State Bank. https://www.happybank.com/resources/six-steps-to-creating-a-positive-money-mindset

Hasty, A. (2023, April 5). *Bank accounts for teens*. Compare the Market. https://www.comparethemarket.com/current-accounts/content/kids-teens-current-accounts/

Hayes, A. (2020, October 3). *Mutual fund*. Investopedia. https://www.investopedia.com/terms/m/mutualfund.asp

Hayes, A. (2022, July 6). Stock. Investopedia. https://www.investopedia.com/terms/s/stock.asp

Jordan, T. (2019, January 14). *The 7 best budgeting methods*. Atypical Finance. https://www.atypicalfinance.com/7-best-budgeting-methods/

Kagan, J. (2023, April 4). *What is an ATM and how does it work?* Investopedia. https://www.investopedia.com/terms/a/atm.asp#:~:text=To%20use%20an%20ATM%2C%20you

Lahunou, I. (2022, June 14). *How to shop smart: 30 ways to make smarter decisions*. Monetha. https://www.monetha.io/blog/rewards/how-to-shop-smart/

Lake, R. (2020, February 4). *How to protect your online banking information*. Forbes Advisor. https://www.forbes.com/advisor/banking/how-to-protect-your-online-banking-information/

Lake, R. (2021, April 9). *What are the different types of bank accounts?* Forbes Advisor. https://www.forbes.com/advisor/banking/what-are-the-different-types-of-bank-accounts/

Langager, C. (2022, August 23). *A beginner's guide to stock investing*. Investopedia. https://www.investopedia.com/articles/basics/06/invest1000.asp

PSECU. (2020, June 5). *How to make good purchasing decisions*. Blog. psecu. https://blog.psecu.com/learn/financial-tips-for-every-stage-in-life/2020/06/05/how-to-make-good-purchasing-decisions

Resnick, N. (2017, July 25). *The 6 best jobs for teenage entrepreneurs.* Entrepreneur. https://www.entrepreneur.com/starting-a-business/the-6-best-jobs-for-teenage-entrepreneurs/296365

Step Change Team. (n.d.). *Credit card debt. what to do if you can't pay.* stepchange. Www.stepchange.org. https://www.stepchange.org/debt-info/credit-card-debt.aspx

Waugh, E. (2022, January 31). *Why is credit important? - experian.* Www.experian.com. https://www.experian.com/blogs/ask-experian/why-is-credit-important/

Which Team. (2023, May 16). *17 ways to save money on your household bills and living costs in 2023 - which?* News. Which? https://www.which.co.uk/news/article/how-to-save-money-on-your-household-bills-aiTGN6b5jZ2N

Wu, A. (2023, May 2). *How to compare prices online (with pictures) - wikiHow life.* Www.wikihow.life. https://www.wikihow.life/Compare-Prices-Online

Financial Literacy for Young Adults

Aspiriant. (13 June 2017). *Making It On Your Own: Taxes.* Aspiriant. https://aspiriant.com/fathom/making-it-on-your-own-taxes/

Baker, B. (13 December 2023). *6 Best Investments For Beginners.* Bankrate. https://www.bankrate.com/investing/best-investments-for-beginners/

Blaine, T. (8 January 2024). *Budgeting For Young Adults: 19 Money Saving Tips For 2024.* Stash. https://www.stash.com/learn/budgeting-for-young-adults/

Boyington, A. (1 June 2023). *How To Do Your Taxes.* Accounting. https://www.accounting.com/resources/how-to-do-taxes/

Carol Dweck: *A Summary Of Growth And Fixed Mindsets.* FS. https://fs.blog/carol-dweck-mindset/

Chen, J. (7 March 2023). *Risk-Return Tradeoff: How The Investment Principle Works.* Investopedia. https://www.investopedia.com/terms/r/riskreturntradeoff.asp

Clear, J. *The Compound Effect By Darren Hardy.* James Clear. https://jamesclear.com/book-summaries/the-compound-effect

Connett, W. (10 July 2022). *10 Steps To Financial Security Before Age 30.* Investopedia. https://www.investopedia.com/articles/younginvestors/08/generation-y.asp

Cruze, R. (29 December 2023). *How To Set Financial Goals: 6 Steps.* Ramsey Solutions. https://www.ramseysolutions.com/personal-growth/setting-financial-goals

Debt.com. (10 January 2923). *Good Debt Vs Bad Debt.* LinkedIn. https://www.linkedin.com/pulse/good-debt-vs-bad-debt-com/

Fontinelle, A. (14 March 2024). *8 Financial Tips For Young Adults.* Investopedia. https://www.investopedia.com/articles/younginvestors/08/eight-tips.asp

GFOA. (4 March 2022). *Long-Term Financial Planning.* GFOA. https://www.gfoa.org/materials/long-term-financial-planning

Gorton, D. (22 December 2023). *Taxes Definition: Types, Who Pays, And Why.* Investopedia. https://www.investopedia.com/terms/t/taxes.asp

Heger, E. (24 February 2024). *Personal Finance 101: Budgeting Basics.* Synchrony. https://www.synchronybank.com/blog/budgeting-basics/

Horton, M. (5 March 2024). *What Are Some Ways To Minimize Tax Liability?* Investopedia. https://www.investopedia.com/ask/answers/040715/what-are-some-ways-minimize-tax-liability.asp

Izad, S. (31 May 2023). *The Importance Of Financial Planning And Retirement Planning: Failing To Plan Is Planning To Fail.* LinkedIn. https://www.linkedin.com/pulse/importance-financial-planning-retirement-failing-plan-sam-izad/

Kagan, J. (28 February 2024). *Taxation Defined, With Justifications And Types Of Taxes.* Investopedia. https://www.investopedia.com/terms/t/taxation.asp

Kerr, A. (29 February 2024). *Financial Independence, Retire Early (FIRE) Explained: How It Works.* Investopedia. https://www.investopedia.com/terms/f/financial-independence-retire-early-fire.asp

Longgrear, J. (4 May 2023). *How To Manage Work-Life Balance With Multiple Income Streams.* Fast Company. https://www.fastcompany.com/90874827/how-to-manage-work-life-balance-with-multiple-income-streams

Matthews, K. (16 January 2024). *A Beginner's Guide To Investing In The Stock Market.* Fortune Recommends. https://fortune.com/recommends/investing/how-to-start-investing/

Modi, P. (19 December 2023). *The Importance Of Exploring Diverse Income Streams Early In Life.* Education Next. https://www.educationnext.in/posts/the-importance-of-exploring-diverse-income-streams-early-in-life

Mukherji, S. (27 August 2023). *The Ultimate Guide: How To Achieve Financial Freedom Before 30.* LinkedIn. https://www.linkedin.com/pulse/

ultimate-guide-how-achieve-financial-freedom-before-30-sujoy-mukherji/

PowHERhouse Money Coaching. (13 March 2023). *5 Tips To Manage Student Debt.* LinkedIn. https://www.linkedin.com/pulse/5-tips-manage-student-debt-powherhouse-money-coaching/

See, B. (31 March 2023). *The Side Hustles 2023: Exploring The Growing Trend Of Independent Work.* LinkedIn. https://www.linkedin.com/pulse/side-hustles-2023-exploring-growing-trend-independent-bobby-see/

Sharma, V. (14 April 2023). *The Magic Of Compounding – Making Money Work For You.* LinkedIn. https://www.linkedin.com/pulse/magic-compounding-making-money-work-you-vaibhav-sharma/

SJB Global. (13 December 2023). *Financial Mindset.* SJB Global. https://sjb-global.com/financial-mindset/

Slifka, R. (6 November 2023). *15 Quotes About Finance From Money-Saving Experts.* Chime Money Moves. https://www.chime.com/blog/15-quotes-from-our-favorite-money-saving-experts/

Tax Deductions And Credits For Young Adults. H&R Block. https://www.hrblock.com/tax-center/filing/adjustments-and-deductions/tax-deductions-for-young-adults/

Taxes Quotes. Brainy Quote. https://www.brainyquote.com/topics/taxes-quotes

Understanding Risk Management In Finance. AccountsIQ. https://www.accountsiq.com/accounting-glossary/understanding-risk-management-in-finance/

Verma, E. (5 March 2024). *What Is Financial Risk And Its Types? Everything You Need To Know.* Simplilearn. https://www.simplilearn.com/financial-risk-and-types-rar131-article

Wealthwrite Company. (20 October 2023). *Role Of Emergency Funds In Financial Security.* LinkedIn. https://www.linkedin.com/pulse/role-emergency-funds-financial-security-wealthwrite-company-msmwc/

What Are The Best Practices For Developing A Long-Term Financial Plan? LinkedIn. https://www.linkedin.com/advice/0/what-best-practices-developing-long-term-financial-nmp9f

Yu, J. (26 February 2024). *5 Basic Methods For Risk Management.* Investopedia. https://www.investopedia.com/articles/investing-strategy/082816/methods-handling-risk-quick-guide.asp

Printed in Dunstable, United Kingdom

75381510R00141